Raffled @ The Bear
Northampton.

Spit 'n' Sawdust Reunion.
2022.

Hope you enjoy the Revised Edition.

All The Best.

Mudge.

Smudge 37 - AKA Mark Eagle
444455

2017

A ROYAL ANGLIAN. Memoirs of a Soldier 1975-1986..

mark eagle smith

1/1/2017

1. MEMOIRS OF A SOLDIER...

FORWARD.

Before I continue, I will say that where possible I have split the book in to paragraphs for each posting or theatre in chronological order or to the best of my knowledge and memory. I have taken memories or events and stories from each one, and my aim is to give as much detail as possible. At the end the book I have listed military wording etc., I unfortunately must use the odd swear word where it was needed or indeed spoken. I will include pictures as much as possible to give authenticity, however some will have to be researched. The names of all characters are real, though abbreviated, why would they not be! Please read on!!

Well I have decided to write my story thus far, concentrating on my military career, from the start in Rothwell at a young age to present day.

The biggest and most rewarding time of my life came in 1974, just turned sixteen years of age and about to leave school. Got a decent job as an apprentice welder on the A6 towards Kettering. But after a while was bored so decided to join the Army. What could be hard about that? See the world and meet people and take in some of the sights.

Anyway, my brother was already in and was always" bigging" it up, so off I went to the careers office in Kettering. Memories of this are little sketchy but nice guys and sent me for selection to Leicester. Had a couple of days there and was accepted in!! Whoopee am off to a flyer.

Richard, my brother had been in a while, he started as a cook in the A.C.C and then later in the R.C.T, and for all the doubters he did his time on active service! he gave me valuable advice and made my list of options as follows; 1. A.C.C

2. R.C.T, 3. Infantry.

The letter finally arrived I had passed, it was the infantry for me....

Excited and worried at the same time! Decided I need to get myself fit and prepare a little as had no idea of anything military apart from what Richard had told me. Fitness was never a problem for me as later in the book explains why. Got a short haircut and read a little from the various paper work they give you and was of the attitude that I would give it time and see how things progressed.

Before I continue I shall give you an insight as to life as it was before joining the army in September 1975.

Pre- ARMY.

Grew up in Rothwell a small Northamptonshire town about 5 miles from Kettering and twenty miles from Northampton. A rural midland town surrounded by gently rolling hills and country lanes, the population of the town was I estimate around 15,000 souls. A mixture of mainly terraced council housing and new developments popping up for, at the time, quite modern, two, three or even four-bedroom houses and of course a scattering of farm houses and indeed working farms in the local area. A small town where everyone knew each- other and it was always good to keep up with the local gossip. A decency amongst people that is rare today. When a neighbour would bring your washing in from the clothes line if rain suddenly appeared. No need for locked doors, people were trust-worthy, and respect was shown to adults and especially the elderly.

A normal and I suppose average school life, not too many friends. But lived for football, day night and at weekends. We played sun, rain, hail or snow! We also would build our own cycles, all second hand of course, however I do remember getting a now most sought- after Chopper Bike for Christmas, some surprise that was believe me, not much money around for expensive toys or bikes then. We would also build our own "Soap Boxes" or "Go Carts" I think we called them then. On leaving school most would usually, go to one of the many Boot and Shoe factories in the area. Northamptonshire was famed for it back then. The two names that stand out are or were Groocock,s and Clarks. Not so many of them now though.

PICS of Rothwell

We were always taught right from wrong, respect and manners and discipline to an extent. There was never much excitement around and now sixteen was looking to escape. A nice village size town, in the heart of Northamptonshire, where everybody knew each other pretty much and life was good, we were a large family so always something going on at home. Not well off but Mum always managed to get us through. Mum and Dad split up when I was around 9 years old, he used to visit every couple of weeks, but this petered out as we grew older. Mum got together with a guy named Brian, they stayed together until Mum passed away, maybe a year after, sadly he took his own life, my brother Richard found him, he had changed a lot since losing Mum, the Doctors say he just missed her so much and could not face life without her. My brothers and I would try and get him out for a drink, but he lost interest in that too. A decent man and step-father to us all.

At school I was average I guess, missed the last 6 months on and off to look after Mum, she had a bad fall so had to take care of the house and generally do everything she could not, at age 15, but I was not stupid either. A few friends I could count on one hand. Wasn't a drinker, as I preferred to keep fit. Had a girlfriend or two but nothing too serious as we just kids, and part of the growing up process I suppose.

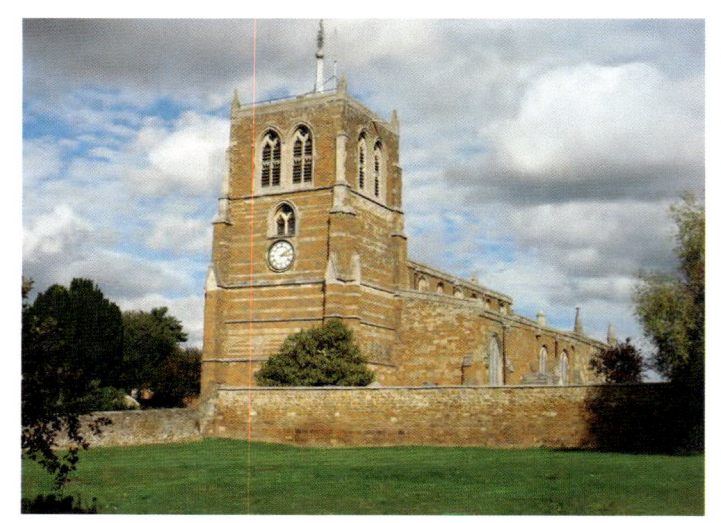

So, it was football in the Mounts, a small park where we all used to gather for football, bikes and general messing about, football was my biggest love at this time and we played morning, noon and night and believe me we played some excellent games. I recall one time when the men from the local foundry works, next to the park used to come over and take us on, boys against men, not a chance, we were pretty good back then. We used to go almost every week to watch Rothwell Town on Saturday, plus we had our own local team, Jubilee Street Rovers was the team name I think? We had a manager and played on Sundays. I remember once the team having its result in the Pink paper, a local rag for the Sports, and was fantastic to see. Am sure it read Jubilee Street Rovers 2- Whoever-0. Great stuff, and like all kids wanted to be a footballer. Wasn't a bad player either, on the wing a la George Best!

Didn't get the chance though.

Got a job as an apprentice welder at a small garage on the A6, now a McDonalds, it was a small family run business and good, honest hard -working people. Electric arc welding was my job and enjoyed it to an extent but was going to take time to qualify. Also I would have needed to study to make it.

Remember walking home from work one Thursday and decided to go to the Army careers office.

From the pictures you get the feel of the place we called home, life was simple and then I got the chance to move on. Had not ventured far from home as back in the eighties it wasn't as easy as today. But a big -change was coming for sure.

One of the low points of those early years was the death of my brother Steven, we shared the same bedroom at home. Steven was a quite lad, well-mannered and a wizard for all things electrical, must have got this knowledge from our Dad a television engineer. He would love the technology of today and would have made a computer programmer or something similar. Steve and I were both smokers and would very often pool our resources for a packet of five Park Drive tipped! Mostly of course the cheap option was tobacco and papers.

Steve wasn't a sporty type like me he was more hands- on with all thing electrical and very clever. He would be in our bedroom for hours stripping down old transistor radios and re building with a better reception and sound! Radio Caroline if I remember correctly. He would have loved the technology of today and I would imagine him to be a game developer or some such career.

We were a big family so bedroom space was at a premium, two sisters and five brothers crammed in to a mid-terrace house, but we managed it. However, in Steve and my room the bed was tight to the bedroom door so could not open it fully as his bed was directly behind it. He was smoking in bed and fell asleep and need I say more. All I can remember is the fire engines and plenty of screaming, shouting and crying. Am sure the local Doctor gave us all a sleeping pill or something. It was a terrible night and will stay with all of us forever I am sure.

So obviously the house was fire damaged and the council decided to put us all in the Rothwell House Hotel, not bad the details are sketchy but am sure we were there for a couple of months. We finally got re-housed in Meadow Road.

Anyway, Steven is on my mind on a daily- basis and will never forget about him. I drive past Jubilee St almost every day. I think of him almost every day, how he would have matured and probably have been a wizard at all thing electrical. As I mentioned before, I am sure he would have made a career in the electrical business, even another Dyson type of inventor even. I hope there is something afterwards because I so want to see him again and tell him how I missed him, we were close and he was a really calm type of person, a cool dude really. It was great to share the room with him.

If there is such thing as Heaven I am certain he will be responsible for lighting the place up!!

Rothwell House Hotel.

Was a difficult and stressful time for all of us, and especially for Mum, but being a big family really helped and of course life went on. We supported each other.

I was fourteen when Steven died so another year rolled by and to bring you back up to date around this time, I left school and landed my first job. Believe it was eighteen pounds and a few shillings a week. Not a bad wage really considering I was not the cleverest and better than being in a shoe factory all day. However, boredom soon set in, wanted more than this. Richard steered me towards the military when he came on leave, pretty-soon decided I would like to give it a go.

Well it's the Army for me then.

Really cannot remember much about the selection only that it was a couple of days away at Leicester? Of course, the army want you to join so it was all positive and easy- going, just had to do a couple of tests like, basic mathematics and questionnaires. All of the staff were very helpful, especially In the early days, and everyone mixed in and chatted about which branch of the Army they would like to join. At the time I thought that being a guardsman would be pretty- cool, Guarding Buckingham Palace seemed to appeal, apparently though, I was too short! On the other hand, patrolling in the jungle Returned home excited and hoped I would be accepted.

The letter did arrive, and I had made it! Couldn't wait to get started and was to report to I.J.L.B, Sir John Moore Barracks in Shorncliffe, Folkestone. The exact dates I forget now, around early September 1975, but excited, nervous and full of hope. I think the travel warrant came in with the letter, the first of many.

So on to the train and was pleased as a couple of guys who had been in Leicester were on the train, there was quite a few joining that day. Mostly nervous chat and made a friend called "Scratch", Mark R being his real name, he came from Northampton, we just got on well and decided we would stick together once we arrived. We went through the whole thing pretty much together unscathed.

I.J.L.B. 1975.

After the War the camp was known as the **Sir John Moore Barracks** and from 1967 it was home to the Junior Infantryman's Battalion (JIB) and later, the Infantry Junior Leaders Battalion (IJLB) until the dissolution of junior soldier recruitment in 1991. The Barracks were then used by regular infantry battalions. When, The Light Infantry moved out in October 1986 the name was retained.

Infantry Junior Leaders Battalion.   Location in Kent.

Well what a shock to the system! Firstly, given forms to fill in, then report to get your equipment and uniform, before going in they gave us our Army number 2438**** was mine, didn't even have time to write it down. By the time we all had our gear and bed space it was back out and learn how to form three ranks. Then off for a haircut, thought mine was short enough. Wrong, short back and sides soon followed.

Shouting, calling names and numbers we were mesmerised! We wondered what hit us, but all worked together and helped with uniforms, as some of the guys were cadets before joining. The staff taught us everything from bed blocks to ironing a shirt, how your locker should look with all uniform folded away nine by nine in its place. How to shape your beret and present yourself, how to address the staff. From this moment on we would double everywhere, that means run. This had to be in the precise and military way, as was almost all movement around camp.

Learning how to march or drill, being the correct military wording, was an eye opener, more to it than meets the eye. But when carried out correctly looks fantastic and I don't believe that any other Army in the world could come anything close to the way we do it! It is all done by numbers and perfect timing, every movement had to be precise. The drill instructors were immaculate not a hair out of place. We had to be the exact, but believe me it takes plenty of time and so much practise to get to a presentable level, that is without a weapon to carry. Drill lessons were hard and repetitive until you got it right. But once right there is no better sight than an infantry Platoon at Present Arms to the shoulder, one of, if not the best drill movement in the book. Also, the sight of a Platoon or Company marching on a full parade all in perfect unison. Great stuff.

The training was hard and you had to learn real fast, if someone was struggling then we all helped out one way or another, especially the fitness, now I thought I had trained enough in my short time before joining up, Wrong, it was really demanding and for a little skinny kid like me, even harder, however there was always someone worse off, the guys who were carrying a little extra weight also suffered and in the main those who suffered most did not make the grade. My way of thinking was that I did not want to end up like those guys, shouting and screamed at and almost being dragged up the hills by the instructors, no Sir not me I will keep going no matter what! Use their failure as a reason to keep up. Anyway, the trick is to pace yourself and overcome the pain, simple as that. This not only applied in training but also carried over to Battalion life in general. Because it can still get hard at times.

On the train down to Folkestone when on leave one time, I thought it would be cool to look out of the window from the train. The next day on the drill square I had a cold in my eyes and could hardly look up, my eyes were streaming tears, the drill instructor was right in my face screaming "What are you Fucking crying for boy, I'm your mother now"!! "Now get on the floor and give me twenty push ups or I will stick this pace stick up your arse and march you round like a fucking lollipop". Trying to explain was useless and the expletives they could rattle off were unbelievable. You never answered back or worse would follow.

Trying not to laugh I duly carried out my twenty, then he was on to the next guy.

The fitness regime never stopped, but pretty much every day we would do the "Hospital Hill" run, this was a killer and caught out many of the undesirables for sure. My trick was to take notice of what was going on around me and just keep going as much as it hurt, legs burning and chest pounding, I felt sorry for some of the lads who really tried but just couldn't run. Their time was up.

Our first night out on the training area soon came, as far as I can remember it was quite tame for what was to come later in my career. We were in combat uniform, obviously, but we did carry all of our gear, webbing, back packs, doss bags and all equipment how they had taught us, not sure we were issued weapons at this time? Well it was a bit of a jolly and quite relaxed, we were taught how to construct a" basha" or bivouac. A small one-man tent if you like, just enough to get you and your gear in, about two feet off the ground fixed between trees with bungee ties or rope. Then you had to camouflage it. Off we all went and the staff would come around and check how we had done.

They said now gather round a large fire and we all had a beer and a sing song. This is where we learnt a few of the old Army songs the generally get belted out when pissed or in good spirits. The fellow Pompadours out there will know what I mean.

At about three o clock in the morning when the rain was bucketing down, all was good, not too many leaks just a damp patch here or there, and at about this time the staff paid us all a visit and I am sure cut all the ropes to everyones basha and we were drenched. They woke us all up shouting how bad we were, told us our attempts were crap and we needed to make them again. By the time all this was done a few times and about one hours sleep later, it was almost daylight and we had breakfast, doubled down this track to meet the Four tonners to take us back to camp. All of us were totally knackered and couldn't wait to get on the trucks. The message came through that the trucks had broken down and we had to "tab" it back to camp.

Am sure this was a ten-mile hike with all gear, the first of many. It was all to test us who could handle it and weed out the no hopers, we lost quite a few that night, I kid you not, the pain when you have a webbing belt digging in to your shoulder and rubbing your skin off is not great, fix that, ok and now I have a blister on my little toe! Just forget it there is no time to stop, got to keep plodding on, ignore the pain, grit your teeth and get on with it, I think Scratch and I looked around the next morning and more than half the intake were gone! Shit we were still here…

Army Basha

A "basha" can be a waterproof canvas or plastic sheet with eyelets or loops along the outside edge. Bashas can be used when camping, outdoor, or in military situations to provide shelter, shade, camouflage, as the army basha, forms a portable overhead cover or tent or groundsheet. Most often supported with bungee cords or string attached to trees.

Bashas should be lightweight enough to be quickly erected and camouflaged in a pattern suitable to their terrain. A low profile gives a small silhouette and advanced models may be Infra-Red Reflective or IRR.

For the first eight weeks there was no respite, no week end pass or a foot outside the camp gates. I was homesick for a few days but had so much to deal with as a sixteen-year-old. But vowed I would never quit having come this far, learning went on and not just military either we also did some schooling i.e., Maths, English etc. But of course, it went on how to deal with orders, cold, hurting, tiredness, kit inspections, bed blocks, drill, weapons training [we couldn't wait for that one] learning more each day, military etiquette, military history so much to take in but every day was a different challenge.

Typical Locker lay out and Bed Block.

A Drill Lesson.

RANGE DAYS.

One of the most important things to learn for all of us was how to fire, strip and assemble, clean and produce accurate fire of our weapons, which included , GMPG, 66mm, 84mm, 9mm Browning Pistol and of course Hand Grenades. So, to this end there were plenty of range days at Hyde ranges[I am sure that was the ranges we used], where we had to "Zero" in our personal weapons, so as to be more accurate when firing, this is basically firing a group, inspect the target and adjust sights as required. Then do it all again!

On a personal note, I really liked the range days and, of course, included was the fabulously famous range stew, A four tonner arrives and the cooks jump out, set up a line of Food Urns normally consisting of potato, stew, carrots, apple pie, custard or rice pudding and we all line up, with mess tins in hand, and proceed along the line filling mess tins at each Urn, Yummy. I recall one day I only had one mess tin so along the line I had stew and potato, and just put the apple pie and custard on top, that day I had desert before my main meal! And I cleaned the mess tin completely, you get hungry on range days.

Also, we had to take our turn in the "Butts", which is down at the target end of the range, as well as lifting "targets up" and "targets down" there was a bucket full of patches and sloppy paste to cover up the bullet holes ready for the next "targets up". It can be hard work in the Butts and If I remember correctly it was a whistle blast for the up and down order, so that all targets were raised and lowered in perfect unison.

To fire these weapons was quite daunting at first, but practise makes perfect, and let us not pretend here, you are no good as an infantry soldier if you cannot hit a target at distance! The first time I fired the SLR I will always remember the kick in the shoulder, after that first one I made sure I done everything I had been taught and really got a good grip, better results instantly, once perfected this is an awesome weapon, when you hit a target with the SLR it stays hit, a 7.62mm round can do plenty of damage.

Another personal favourite is the GPMG, I would say that but then so would most other infantry soldiers, another fantastically accurate and very effective machine gun, I still think it is used today?

The 66mm and 84mm are anti-tank weapons, the 66 is a throw away once fired and is pretty basic, pull it open, line up the shot and fire, pretty effective though against soft skin vehicles. But the 84mm Carl Gustav now that is better, same principle but is reloadable and a great asset to the section in case of Tank threat. It can be fired by one but is most effective with a two-man team, one to load and one to fire. We fired both on a live firing range and was great to get the experience.

Also, the Hand Grenade, again there is a technique for throwing these things, and it works, self-explanatory, and does the job for FIBUA and in most clearance operations. Again, we did throw live grenades and added it to our experience.

Yes, we had some great days at the ranges, however, every now and again, especially in the early days, there would be a break down in the transport, so we had to "tab" it back to camp. This was done to improve getting used to all the equipment we had to carry over a long distance, and improving stamina and fitness, to be honest the more we done it the easier it was. The aim as with most military things, the more you practise the easier it becomes, I considered myself competent with the SLR and GPMG, I would not be making the Battalion Shooting Team or Sniper Course but not a bad shot.

After a few months, once the numbers had been reduced significantly, we felt we had earned more respect from the instructors, they were still hard but seemed happier with those of us that were left.

We were given tasks both as a team or individually and were given time a s squad leader or 2.I.C. second in command. We learnt to be a team and work for each other which at the end of the day is what it was all about. If you were told to do something, you done it to the best of your ability.

Coming home on leave one time, I came from St Pancras station in London to get to Kettering to home and was that knackered that I fell asleep on the train and woke up in Leicester, luckily my Dad picked me up, I know my brother Richard had been in for some-time but Dad was proud of me I think. I had not seen my father in a number of years until that day, without hesitation he instantly said stay put and I will pick you up from the station. We spoke once more after that at my brother David's house, quite some time after I had left the Army, again dates are a little hazy but around the year two thousand, I think. He was in a bad way and had bone Cancer but never complained, we recalled the aforementioned lift home and that we should meet up one more time. It wasn't meant to be, he always kept in contact with my sister Sue. Only a short time after the conversation she had told us he was gone. Shame we never met again. However, we did attend his funeral, and all say our farewells, he was still Dad after all that had happened.

So, life went on at I.J.L.B, it was tough, especially in the early days, as I may have mentioned, repeat, refresh, re-learn and do it all again, and as time moves on you are taught something new every day and believe me there is so much to learn, even just the basics. Of course, only being sixteen at the time, we still had to attend normal lessons, English, Maths, Science were the main subjects as I remember, although there may have been others, one was History and of course Military, related to the units we were to join, re-calling old battles and honours earned by the different Regiments. To be honest the mixture of Lessons and Military worked well, so education also improved as well as the soldiering side of things.

We were getting fit day by day, getting stronger and as the year went by, we turned from boys to men for sure.

Anyway, we made it through the whole thing and at almost seventeen were ready, the passing out parade was a parade and March Past and parents and family came to see us. A great- day, and my Mum had a tear in her eye, she was so proud and let me tell you, so was I. Would have liked for my Father to have be there though.

My last word on I.J.L.B was that I missed the last big Hoorah the end of year "battle camp". Unbeknown to me at the time, this had to be done, so I was told that before I can join the Regiment, I must complete the battle camp at the Queens Division Depot. The reason being I had suspected appendicitis and was sent to Woolwich Military Hospital for two weeks while the others were on battle camp. After two weeks they said no need to have my appendix out so have a week's leave and report to the Depot afterwards.

Woolwich military Hospital was a massive hospital and took care of most of the Army in general, I think? My time there was thankfully short lived, after several tests and plenty of prodding and poking about my stomach it was deemed that no operation was needed at this time so after a couple of weeks, I was discharged with two weeks leave and then onward to the Depot at Bassingbourne.

Whilst at the hospital though, the one thing I remember is that in this hospital there was no need for rank, as we were all in there for various ailments, however there is always one exception to the rule, in this case a big mouthed Army Sergeant Major who made it be known, he was in charge. As I remember he was not an infantry soldier, more like a rear echelon type. Not for long!, A few of us whom had made friends during our small stay decided that we were not happy with this guy, anyway during your stay, there is a rota for tea making and each of us took our turn, we all agreed it is about time he learned his lesson so during my turn one afternoon we had managed to obtain a sachet of laxative and added this to the " big mouth" afternoon cuppa! Well, we were in fits of laughter as after about thirty seconds after drinking his tea, he was up and running for the toilet like a man possessed. After this had happened, two or three times, and as I passed by his bed, I said to him, you really should be a little nicer to the lower ranks "Sir". I think he understood what had happened. I did not get a response as within seconds he was off again heading for the loo!! Never set eyes on him again and was soon off home for a two- week holiday before heading out to the Depot, The Queens Division.

Hello to Royston, Bassingbourne Barracks. Depot the Queens Division. [Guardroom picture below] My God after all I had been through, I virtually had to start again!! Only the last six weeks though. To cut a long story short I survived it, passed with flying colours and yet another passing out parade later I was fit for the regular Army. This part is a real blank, could not even tell you the names of the training Platoon I was in or any names from that time.

The only event that stands out from my time at the Depot , is the memory of a final room inspection and we were getting near to the end of training so everything had to be immaculate, the bed space I was allocated had been vacated by a new recruit who never made the grade, I had never really noticed, as all squaddies have various pictures stuck on to locker doors, usually of scantily clad or half naked girls ,page three, pop idols or exotic cars stuck to their locker with blu-tac or Sellotape, not this guy!

So, with the inspecting group approaching, this includes usually, the O.C, CSM, Platoon Commander, training NCO and other hangers on of varying rank, we were called to, "attention" . I stood to attention, with all of my kit laid out as per normal S.O P,s with my now highly bulled Best Boots at the bottom, of the bed, as the Sergeant Major came nearer to my locker he started shouting " what the fuck is that on your locker", I did not have a clue, then on looking closer, there was a picture of Hitler in uniform in some old picture shaking hands with some dignitary of some description.

The CSM went berserk and started swinging his pace stick around, too close to my head, I quickly grabbed the picture and ripped it off the locker, threw it and it landed next to my Best Boots on the bed, again the CSM started to hit out again with his pace stick and almost hit my boots, again I grabbed for the offending picture and threw it over the locker thus saving my boots from further attack. After that the whole place was in silence, on questioning I explained that having only been there a short time I had not noticed the offending picture and would most certainly have removed it if I had noticed. The Sergeant Major seemed happy with my explanation and to make sure that I found it and disposed of it as soon as possible, he then said my best boots looked very good! That was a close shave and I will never forget the look of anger on his face whilst swinging away with his pace stick. Missing me by millimetres every swing!

Once the inspection had finished and they all left the Barrack room the whole place erupted into fits of laughter and none of us had ever seen anything like it on an inspection, before or since, I had to tell my fellow trainees I honestly did not notice the picture stuck on my locker, and maybe the outgoing guy had left it on my locker on purpose!

The other stand -out memory from the Depot was the Log runs, ask any soldier that has took part in one of these and he will tell you it Is hard training. Basically the "log" is a telegraph pole, that is it. Each soldier takes his position according to height, if not the short man in the middle does not even touch the thing never mind use any effort. But it is running with it over varying distances also completing sit -ups or other exercises with the log, not very pleasant at all, you certainly feel satisfaction if you can last the pace, timing needs to be perfect for switching the log from one shoulder to the other and perfect unison when carrying out sit -ups. Not to forget the obstacles you need to get over and of course the deep mud filled water holes to run through. But nonetheless a perfect way of training for an Infantry Soldier. Hard, Hell yes, but rewarding and a great sense of achievement, and like most aspects of Physical training, the more you carry out these tasks, the easier it becomes.

So yes, a short period of training here to complete my basic training that had started a year before as a Junior Soldier in Sir John Moore barracks in Folkestone. I was pleased to get through, but there was no Family at the final Passing Out parade as had already done that at I.J.L.B. Of course, the parade went well and then it was a matter of time before we all joined our different Battalions, a mix of mainly Royal Anglians, and Royal Regiment of Fusiliers.

However, I had to wait for a flight out to Cyprus which would be my first posting.

Guardroom, Bassingbourne Barracks.

While waiting I was posted to A company, not sure exactly, as a Company runner. Enter in to my life one Sgt Major M! A most excellent soldier and always immaculately turned out. I wanted to be this guy, he was, and I mean no disrespect, the perfect military clockwork soldier, but whatever you do not wind him up! He had control of everything and you could never get away with even a shirt button out of place. The bellowing voice shouting "Runner" still makes me shiver to this day.

Never at any time did I miss one command of "Runner" and was always immaculate in my appearance, it was great preparation for the time ahead.

Every time he shouted "Runner" I had to bang my tabs in and be immaculate. One day "RUNNER" he almost screamed it, I duly doubled in and banged to attention "Sir", he said run to the N.A.A.F.I and get me a tube of fucking toothpaste and one tin of polish, it's a fucking emergency! Yes, Sir I replied right turned and banged my right foot in, hard, and marched off. Once out of the office it suddenly dawned on me, I have no money on me, Shit, I got to go and ask him for some. After a couple of minutes, I plucked up the courage, fearing the worst, and knocked on his office door "Enter" banged my tabs in again, He bellowed "Are you still here! Here's the fucking money soldier" as he slammed a note on the desk, one more deep breath and he said" all things considered shit for brains you will be an asset to your Regiment, now get out of my office before I change my mind". I was gone and as proud as hell!

My last word on this soldier was that one morning he ordered me to bring him a tea to his room at 06.00hrs. Some big Parade or something, I barely slept fearing if I was late that would be my career over. Arrived with the tea as ordered and to my surprise he answered the door in Army green "grots" and vest and to my amazement they were immaculately pressed even starched I reckon with creases like in perfect position!! Amazing.

I had the utmost respect for this Sergeant Major, all things considered he was always fair and treated everyone the same. I had learned so much about discipline in that short space of time, as I used to watch and listen all the time, the way he dealt with certain situations and the form of punishment always fitting the "crime". For example if it was a dress code thing it was normally a "Bollocking" and put on report, so the Section Commander could deal with it, if it was down to sloppiness in dress , then more practise on turn out and parading at different times in different uniforms, if reported for laziness or idleness, then extra Drill will do the job. A stereo typical ols school Sergeant Major, scary yet approachable, just.

I joined I.J.L.B as a boy soldier, completed my final 6 weeks exercise at the Depot Queens Division and was now joining the Battalion as a regular. I finally made it, well almost…

CYPRUS Tour 1976   / U.N Tour 1980.

I have incorporated the United Nations tour alongside our tour in 1976 where we were a resident Battalion, along with a return U.N Tour in 1980. I think that the two go pretty much together. The first posting was for a resident Battalion on the Island, this was more of a presence on the island, we trained just as a normal infantry battalion would do at home, the second however was as part of the United Nations Peace keeping force, where we wore the Blue beret of the United Nations.

The Background as to why we were here during the United Nations tour is explained in the next paragraph with map also.

"Launched with relatively few troops, the Turkish landing had limited success at first, and resulted everywhere on the island in the occupation of Turkish-Cypriot enclaves by the Greek forces. After securing a more- or less satisfactory bridgehead Turkish forces agreed to a cease-fire on 23 July 1974. The same day civilian government under Karamanlis took office in Athens, the day the Sampson coup collapsed. Glafcos Clerides became the Acting President in absence still of Makarios.

Two days later formal peace talks were convened in Geneva between Greece, Turkey and Britain. Over the course of the following five days Turkey agreed to halt its advance on the condition that it would remain on the island until a political settlement was reached between the two sides. Meanwhile, Turkish troops did not refrain from extending their positions, as more Turkish-Cypriot enclaves were occupied by Greek forces. A new cease-fire line was agreed. On 30 July the powers agreed that the withdrawal of Turkish troops from the island should be linked to a 'just and lasting settlement acceptable to all parties concerned'. The declaration also spoke of 'two autonomous administrations -that of Greek-Cypriot community and that of the Turkish-Cypriot community'. On 8 August another round of discussion was held in Geneva, Switzerland. Unlike before, this time the talks involved the Greek and Turkish Cypriots. During the discussions the Turkish Cypriots, supported by Turkey, insisted on some form of geographical separation between the two communities. Makarios refused to accept the demand, insisting that Cyprus must remain a unitary state. Despite efforts to break the deadlock, the two sides refused to budge. On 14 August, Turkey demanded from Clerides acceptance of a proposal for a federal state, in which the Turkish Cypriot community (who, at that time, comprised about 18% of the population and owned about 10% of the land) would have received 34% of the island. Clerides asked for 36 to 48 hours to consult with the Cypriot and Greek governments, but Turkey refused to grant any consultation time, effectively ending the talks. Within hours, Turkey had resumed its second offensive. By the time a new, and permanent, ceasefire was called 36 per cent of the island was under the control of the Turkish military. The partition was marked by the United Nations Buffer Zone in Cyprus or "green line" running east to west across the island."

One of the observation Post's on the buffer zone.

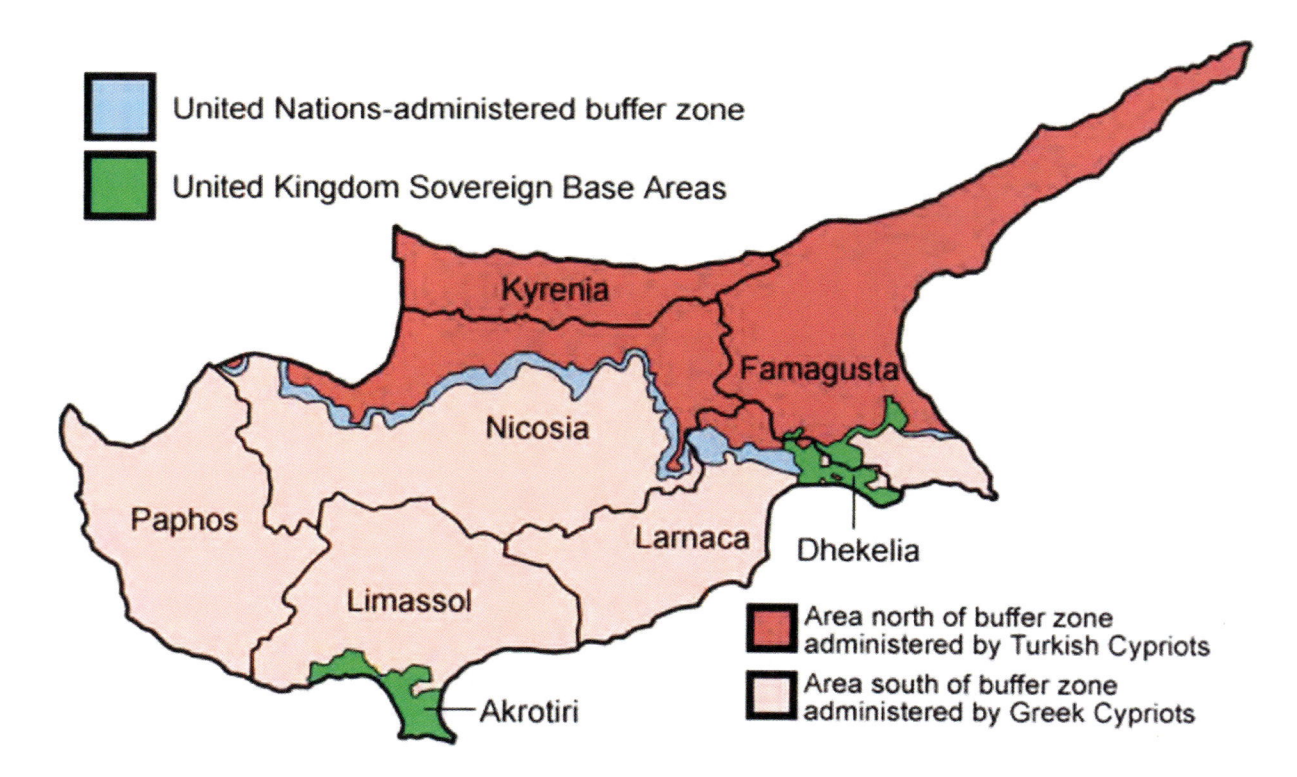

The U.K was having a heatwave though we had one of our own, I remember stepping off from the VC10 and the heat just hitting me! So here I was on my first posting from Junior Leader to Regular soldier and was ready. Would be hard pushed to even consider having a holiday in a place like this. Must have been thirty degrees. But what a beautiful place. More about the Island later.

Shortly after this I was on my way to Cyprus to join the Battalion. Arrived I think in Lightweight combats with all kit, Army suitcase and kitbag.

Dropped off at the guardroom, think by bus, not sure now or even how many of us?

In to the guardroom and banged my tabs in to the guardroom to the Guard commander, Corporal "Monty" B.

Remember here I was, just finished training, ready to go, finely tuned and very fit, ripped I guess they would say now, and ready for anything.

So, marched in and stated" Corporal I am 2438….", he interrupted with, "ok enough of that I am Monty ok." Yes, Corporal I replied, keen to show my Discipline and he interrupted again, "look I am Monty you don't have to keep calling me Corporal your training has finished now, you have been assigned to one platoon, their Block is over there and he pointed the general direction, you need to report their asap. I replied OK Monty, he shouted back 2 that's Corporal to you sprogg!

A complete Brain Freeze what the fuck is happening? Oh well seems I am going to have to get the hang of it somehow, but very hard to understand after the last year.

Anyway, I learnt as the time went on, it is difficult for civvies to understand but you always respect the rank, but also there is a time and a place for it. It takes some time to work it out if I ever really did. But a big thank you to Monty, as am sure he was also my first platoon sergeant? Without his and the rest of the Platoon,s guidance I probably wouldn't have lasted too long. Even now, despite a few different roles within the Battalion these guy's are the ones I cherish most, where it all began, and let me tell you this, these men taught me so much and not once did I feel threatened, bullied or in any way get mistreated. This is the Army for God's sake get on with it! Learning the hard way is possibly the best way to learn, that way you never make the same mistake twice and I had learned that lesson well.

1 Platoon 1976- just joined the Battalion. Me, Centre of picture.

Company Accommodation. [similar]

View from Block to "Choggy" Shop.

Buffer Zone Sign.

On another occasion, I remember area cleaning outside the block area with the rest of the platoon and word came that an R. P was asking for me at the road next to our accommodation block, oh shit what did I get up too? Was worried so doubled up to the road and there stood this R.P staring from under the peaked cap" are you Smith 37" he asked, I replied "Yes Staff". He then shouted "You are in trouble soldier!" then he said it's me Danny S from Rothwell you Pratt! to be honest I never recognised him, just could not put a name to the face, to be honest he knew my brother better, anyway, later he told me he borrowed the R.P, s armband to wind me up. We went to the "choggy shop" for a coffee and egg banjo I think. Still owe him for that one.

He now owns his own successful Pest Control business in Desborough and a great guy and ex-Pompadour. Just slightly before my time. I think I am right in saying that he left shortly after our little meeting.

Typical U.N Observation Post.

Whilst serving I still loved my Sport, and enjoyed football, made it into the Company team, the pic is from Happy Valley where we played. One is getting a runner up medal for I think semi-finals of the Army Cup [we lost]. I came on as a substitute, played left wing, remember making a couple of crosses but alas we lost that one, I also believe it was broadcast on BFPO Radio, would be amazing if a recording of that game turned up somewhere. We had some great players and me being relatively new to the Battalion, the team looked after me well. Yes, they were great days, with great people, there is nothing that compares with the comradeship in the Army. We all would drink and socialise together and live and die together if needed.

We also trained of course, memory fades now but can recall carrying out weapon training and cleaning, the odd drill lesson thrown in for good measure, you never know when the next big parade will come along, so we just basically covering all aspects on a daily basis, patrol techniques and section attacks, mostly carried out on the training area, but also there was plenty of room on camp to carry out the basics, such as weapon training and cleaning, in fact I remember one of my first most important jobs was being sent to the "choggy" shop for the whole section ordering and bringing back egg banjos and teas and such. I did as CPL M instructed, which was do as your told, and keep your mouth shut and listen.

I cannot remember the reason I messed up, but we arrived for some sort of training one day, luckily quite close to camp, and I had forgotten to collect a piece of equipment, well straight away I admitted my mistake, otherwise the whole Platoon would suffer and that is not correct! Anyway, as I recall I had the choice of a smack in the mouth or a 252, which is a formal charge in the military and a blemish on my so far good standing, I took the hit, not that bad, think he held back. And I did have the choice. I found later that a charge against you is a definite pain in the backside. I deserved it, as in a real situation there is no second chances. But our Battalion routine went on, and in the military, you move on and we had plenty of free time for sunbathing and general rest and recuperation.

The island was a beautiful place, and for me never to have hardly ever set a foot outside of the UK, it was an amazing experience, the furthest I had been was Belgium on a school football outing. So to be here was surreal, I had to pinch myself. You can see from a couple of the pictures the scenery was amazing and I will always remember the smell of the orange groves when we were on "exercise"

There was always an "orange " fight whilst we were out and about, some of the oranges were the size of footballs! If you got "hit" you felt it. And of course, a great source of energy or drink when on exercise. And refreshment when playing sport or on a run.

We were based in Limassol, although quite a small town back in 1976 it has grown somewhat, I remember visiting some ancient ruins there, the Kuorion I think is called, there is plenty of ruins to visit all over the island, also Aphrodites birth place. An Ampitheatre I recall, was near- by and of course plenty of Taverns to drop into for a beer, we used to use the Amathus Hotel, this was still being built when we were there, a five star hotel I believe.

I will always remember my best friend at the time "Scratch" and myself heading for the Amathus one night, aiming to chat up the Swedish Ladies that used to holiday there, we never quite made it, as the place was not busy, as we had arrived too early for the nightclub to get in to full swing, we decided to try a couple of shots! Bad idea, I know Scratch started at one end of the bar, and a shot from every bottle there, there must have been twenty different drinks. I carried him back that night.

But most Squaddies, no matter which country they are in, will take in the local culture and visit historical sites and other such places of interest. It is not always drinking time! We also enjoyed and made the most of the island when we had time off. Sometimes though, things went a little too far.

One such event was a few of our guys had hired a speed boat from Limassol Marina, unfortunately, and no names here, they had all had a little too much drink and had got lost, without a care, and a few more beers, they just aimed the speedboat for dry land, right around the tip at Aya Napa and somehow had landed in Famagusta on the Turkish held side of the island. About a sixty kilometre trip, Well, this caused an International Incident at the time, and also made Sky News, the government on both sides had to sort it out, and it made the main news in the U.K, they were accused of being spies, or even being sent by the British Army to "recce" positions, When in reality, it was a couple of drunken soldiers let loose without a map. Finally, the whole incident was played down, and all sides seen the funny side of the event. Those guys, [no names] took a while to get over that one!

Workwise, life went on and I must admit, for my first posting, it was the perfect start, the guys in the Platoon really helped me along and I will take this opportunity to thank them all now. You see, in the Army, you have people leaving and new recruits coming in on a constant basis, and you all have -to stick together to make it work, no bullying in our day, just show the new guys how it works, and it does. The change from Junior Soldier to a fully- fledged member of an Operational Battalion is a complicated but rewarding experience. It only takes time, and you have plenty of time to learn.

Receiving runners up medal? Cyprus 1976 I think? Broadcast on B.F.P.O Radio.

Norman L,? ? Geordie C, Milzarek?, Myself, |?

? ? Titch M, Bob P, Graham H, Bill S, Brian H, Jock B.

So back to the routine again, exact details are a little rusty now, but we patrolled the border or peace line [buffer zone] regularly and carried out normal military duties, but we did have quite a bit of free time too. Mostly on a daily- basis, as after twelve middays it was too hot to work!

I also enrolled on a parachute course at Pergamos, I seem to recall the whole course being run by our very own CPL Mick B, and was accepted, only paid ten Cypriot Pounds per jump. It was a fantastic experience and a real buzz to jump from a perfectly good aircraft, a Cessna 172 if I remember correctly. As always and thankfully we endured a couple of weeks' ground training [Boring] but had to be done and thankfully done right. Our instructor, Mick B{CPL}. A top parachutist too, when it came to the packing of parachutes, we were a little fed up until they said we would be jumping with those the next day. Everyone scrambled them back and double, no triple checked them!!! It was also too windy for novice parachute jumps, so I went to the pool and tried to better myself by learning to swim. {River crossings are quite daunting if you cannot swim}. Still swim like a brick now though. Sure, it helped though. This lasted for only a few days, until the wind had reduced, then we were clear to jump.

Anyway, along came the day for our first jump, you had to climb out on to the step above the wheel and hold on to the cross member for the wing and dangle your leg, when the instructor tapped you, you pushed out and back and adopted the freefall position. WOW! The landing soon came upon you, my God all you could do was steer these parachutes left or right, heading towards the orange groves, I really did not want to end up dangling from an orange tree! Thankfully, I floated over those, but the impact when you hit the ground is harsh, however land as you were taught, and it all comes together nicely. An amazing feeling and was amazed that afterwards Cpl Baxter said I was shit, arms all over the place, to be honest on that first one you really don't know what to expect, got better after that and by the tenth jump was ready for dummy pull's, that is still on a static line but you go through the process of pulling the rip cord and should be in your hand when you hit the deck. I would recommend anyone to try it as is very exhilarating.

One morning the old caravan or shack we used to have a brew and wait for the next jump, was burnt to the ground, being a cigarette- smoker the finger was pointed at me, but I swear to this day. Not Guilty Cpl B.

Yes, a fantastic posting for my first one overseas, I also had my welcome or should I say induction into the Battalion there, but the details will remain private, suffice it to say not a very nice thing but hey when you're in your in, and if you can't handle that you really shouldn't be there in the first place. But this would definitely not be classed as bullying.

In a short space of time I learnt to be a pretty good rifleman and settled in to the Battalion and was pleased with the way it was all going.

On the grapevine was that our next posting would be Northern Ireland, no not yet, surely.

Yes, 1978 was a busy year for us in Cyprus, operationally we were scattered all over the island, Troodos about 6,000 feet up in the clouds, Ayious - Nikolaious near Famagusta, and our own camp at Episkopi, training also takes us to Pyla Ranges, near Larnaca Bay and also as far North as Akamas, a forgotten peninsular, not that far from Turkey.

I remember as part of our training in 77, we carried out Inter Platoon Battle Test in form of a competition, July if I recall, and one of the hottest on record! We concentrated on shooting and other basic skills, the test itself was an Inspection after which we were moved by vehicles, then we were ambushed, and then we had a " TAB" Tactical Advance to Battle, or forced march of 11 Kilometers, carrying all of our equipment, which weighed in at a hefty 60-80lbs! in 100 degree heat!!, we guzzled water every step of the way. This was swiftly followed by us setting our own ambush and finally we "tabbed" another 4 miles this time "speed march" to the end of exercise on the ranges at Akrotiri. I am at a loss as to where we ended up, but I think Recce Platoon won it? Hard and gruelling, but we loved it. Every platoon took part and I believe there were a couple of high profile dignitary,s attending, whom were mightily impressed.

Being a "sprog" or newcomer to the Battalion I got my head down and got on with it, with great mates and team-work we all made it through, Great memories that will never fade. However, the officer in charge had taken us on the "tab" I am sure he took us through the same village two or three times, I remember saying to one of the lads "we have been here before..fucking twice already" he agreed, but we kept on with the "tab". Officers are never very good with maps.

Fancy "tabbing" 10 miles in this? In 35 degrees heat!

Valletta, Capital of Malta.

On the 11th January we visited Malta on Operation Turnabout, we were housed at Ghajn Tuffieha Barracks North of Golden Bay via RAF Luqa. Here we trained to practise our shooting skills and carry out minor exercises at Hal Far airfield. We were assisted by 41 Commando and taught familiarisation in Gemini Assault Boats and Gazzelle Helicopters. Also, Rock climbing and survival training with 41 Commando.

Above. On the chopper, off the chopper. Malta - Jan.1977? [not sure on date] Training with 41 Commando Royal Marines.

I recall on our R AND R time in Malta, we visited a church I think in Valletta? the capital, the Mosta Dome Church, which had been bombed during the World War, however, in this particular church the bomb had not exploded, and it was still in the exact spot it had dropped in to, and the church was now a major tourist attraction. I must say a beautiful church, I remember especially, the pattern of squares on the ceiling. The roof was a massive dome shape, it was pleasing that the bomb never exploded and ruined a perfect and such a beautiful building.

Troodos Mountain Range.

A long hot -summer for sure, however for our hard -work we were rewarded with nights out in historic Valletta and medieval Rabat. Two weeks hard training and plenty learnt was soon over and returned to Cyprus a couple of weeks later and wiser!

On one crazy night out after a hard -day training we all decided that we would have a couple of drinks in the N.A.A.F.I then head in to town for one of the Night-clubs [what could possibly go wrong].

We, being about 10 or 12 in number were having a great night, after the N.A.A.F.I we had a few in the local "pubs" before the night-club. We arrived at The Famous Kings Disco!, a little too early, as the place was almost empty, anyway, we sank a few more beers and all of a sudden the place started to fill, squaddies always liked to chat up and keep friendly with the locals, however it all got out of hand when some local guy tried to sit on Steve N,S knee, after a couple of warnings the guy was duly clobbered by Steve, with that all hell broke loose and the local Cypriot,s just came from no-where and one hell of a fight ensued! We gave some and received a few knocks ourselves, but we managed to escape down the stairs to the exit, why was I the last one, anyway we ran into the street and the punch-up continued, we were vastly out-numbered.

I tripped on the kerb, and was immediately surrounded, being kicked all-over, protected myself as best I could, covering my head with my arms, at that precise moment the Police arrived, as the locals backed off and I looked up from the floor all I could see was these mates of mine waving and cheering saying "Come on Smudge- you are doing great!" they were about one hundred yards away on the other side of the street! Really!. I escaped with only bumps and bruises.

What a mess, we were all arrested by the local Police and taken down to the station, we were shoved in to Land-rovers and the Police followed on behind, 2 Land-rovers and 2 Police cars, Volkswagen Beetles I remember, one of my mates, Kev B said to me he was already in trouble and the R.S.M had warned him, one more slip-up and you WILL be locked up.

As we slowed to take a corner in the road, he jumped, rolled onto the ground with a parachute roll and ran. The convoy stopped, and the Police suddenly pulled out their Pistols and started waiving them around! They gave -up looking for Kev and followed us the rest of the way with pistol pointing at us from the car behind. Once we arrived at the cells in the local Police Station, the Duty Guard Commander came from camp, we all had to make statements. By this time it was almost daylight and we marched from the Guardroom to the R.S.M,s office still covered in blood with clothing ripped and black eyes and cuts to almost every-one of us. Most of the Battalion were just awake and heading for breakfast, so all eyes were upon us.

The RSM was not pleased, we did say that they were calling the British Army and in particular our Regiment with a bad name, he kept repeating the question? " who was the one that got away?"

We said we were so drunk "Sir" we honestly cannot remember. To our amazement he let us all off with a warning, and Kev lived to fight another day, if you will excuse the pun.

Yes, in general we all behaved outside of camp, but by the same token we will not let any-one out-fight us either!

Another grand occasion in Cyprus was of course the Queens Silver Jubilee.

As I mentioned earlier, you never know when there is a big parade just around the corner, so drill practise is always useful, get the rust out of us, as we had not drilled for some time, and we had to remember the moves, with weapons. Of course, the Queens Silver Jubilee parade came along, and it is practise drill, more drill, and then some more drill. The lightweight Number 2 dress really helped in that heat. I do not think these look as good as the Number two dress we wear back in the U.K, but extremely comfortable in the heat of the day here.

On the 3rd June the parade was held at Happy Valley, the commander of the parade, Lt Col D paid tribute to the Her Majesty with a 21 Gun Salute from HMS Mohawk, which was anchored in the bay. Will never forget the noise from those guns, as it echoed around the valley! Plus, our own Feu de Joie, this is a rifle salute along the ranks to give a continuous rat- a tat effect. Their was also a Royal Air Force fly-by with a Nimrod, escorted by 3 Canberras, and helicopters. This was followed by the usual march past taken by the Commander British Forces Cyprus, the Air Vice-Marshall.

We were thankful of the lightweight No2 Dress in the heat-of the day but as mentioned but still dripping with sweat, and a great parade to celebrate the Queen in her 25th anniversary.

Queens Silver Jubilee March Past – A company – Happy Valley, Cyprus 1977.

I really enjoyed both tours in Cyprus, and will like to get back there one last time, it was a first look in a foreign country for me and I think most Pompadours would agree a great tour.

So, my first overseas posting came to an end, when we were to move to Bulford, the next posting was to be to Northern Ireland.

We were posted to Bulford/ Tidworth to undergo our N.I Training. 1978.

Really do not remember much about the training, except a mock town where we honed our patrol techniques and were prepared for and practised different scenarios. F.I.B.U.A or fighting in built up areas i.e. coming under fire, ied s, booby traps, riot situations. Most people tend to look inwards or towards a distraction, but you really need to cover your arc of fire and to be constantly observing, doors, windows, and the people around you. We also practised Riot Control, it looks messy but, with training, you can manipulate the rioters in a direction they do not wish to go, thus easing the tension away from the main trouble spot, well at least we would try to accomplish that, however in reality, it is very different. Endless foot patrols around the mock -up streets, which I have to say was realistic, dealing with different scenarios, from booby trap devices, to trying to arrest a known suspect. Of course sometimes we would be in vehicles [Land Rovers [and we also practised patrolling in vehicles, and how to carry out a vehicle check-point, which is a regular occurrence on the streets, when you maybe need to cut off an escape from a known terrorist. We, as always, practised our shooting on an indoor range using Heckler Cock. Two- two rounds. Not bad for the seventies, different films were played and sometimes you hit the good guy [collateral damage]. Again though, practise makes perfect.

All- in- all the training went well and by the time we were due to head to Belfast, we were ready!

NORTHERN IRELAND. 1978-79.

We were posted to Palace Barracks just outside of Belfast, in a town called Hollywood, well for sure this was the real deal, and it was time to earn our pay. Before the posting we were allowed on leave to visit family, and I remember Mum saying that I wasn't allowed to go, I replied try telling that to the sergeant major. No, it was a worrying time for all concerned at the time, seems as if it would just rumble on for years, and that was the case. There were plenty of shootings and bombings on a daily-basis but unlike now, this was never reported in the press or T.V.

I do remember my Mother saying that she did not want me to go to Ireland, there must have been literally thousands of "Mums" up and down the Country all saying the same. Although it was sometimes reported on the news, well the major events anyway, not like today, Mothers knew that there was the chance that her son may not be coming home. I wrote and telephoned from the old phone box, to keep her from worrying too much. We would also write letters home when possible, just to let the family know we were fine, and it was great, so not to worry we would be home in no time at all. Also, that it was really easy, and we were not on the street much, which of course was not true, it put my Mums mind at ease, I think.

The posting was for one and a half years! normally at that time units were sent over to the Province, for four- month tours of duty although they stayed in one place for the duration, in our case it was in to the "Ballymurphy" for a couple or three of weeks at a time and then r +r back at Palace Barracks. This was to be the routine.

Anyway, as an eighteen-year-old I was shitting bricks, not nice to be in fear for your life almost every day. No, it wasn't Afghanistan or Iraq but the same sort of fear, at least in those conflicts they had the chance to return fire. Every patrol you had to be on the ball just do as you practised keep your eyes open and be ready for anything. Can you imagine walking through the streets in an estate in your home town and a sniper opening- up on you or as you walk past a lamp post it blows up. Or two or three masked gun-man jumping out of an alleyway to take a pot shot at you.

P. check.

We had the art of patrolling nailed after a while and it becomes second nature after a couple of times on the street, being the tail end Charlie takes some practice. That is patrolling backwards, and you do rely on your opposite number to make you aware of lamp posts etc.

I.R.A gunman.

You really cannot relax for a second, or shit happens, and you are not ready. Your Dead.

When you stop on patrol, do not stay in the same place for too long, do the unexpected ie. Dart across the road and back to a different position. If you do, crouch for a while balloon. That is move your body and head constantly so if a sniper has you in his sights, he cannot get a shot off. All of this takes communication with other brick members and the truth is you trust these guys with your life and vice versa.

Rioting is also a scary enviroment, and it usually starts from nothing, for instance, while p checking someone, things get a little heated, and before you know it the dustbin lids would start banging, which is a sign to bring out the locals and it soon escalates. Before you know it, a large crowd has gathered, and the younger ones start pelting you with the stones and bottles. Of course, some of these were planned to lure your patrol in to an ambush, and open fire on you.

On one occasion, we were patrolling the "murph" and outside of the shops, I think on Kellys Corner? Our commander spotted a known and wanted I.R.A member, we tried the softly -softly approach but the bastard run like a rabbit, so there is our brick and a street full of them, chasing us, chasing him.

He hid in one of the terraced houses, so Bob Mac kicked the door in and we followed suite, they tried to hide him, but we found him cowering behind a cupboard, then a female with a childs buggy, would stand in our way and block us getting to him. No chance he wasn't getting away. We finally got him onto the street and had already called for back- up, usually a couple of land rovers or a "pig", to pick them up. The street was packed, and we were getting lots of abuse, fuck knows where they all come from, but it really was a big crowd. Only four of us and fifty to seventy screaming civilians, who want to kill you, are getting closer by the minute, is a scary place to be, Bob Mac said if they not here soon, we going to have to let him go. No Chance of that we agreed, a pig arrived in the nick of time. We were expecting to be contacted [fired on] at any minute, but thankfully, it never came. The terrorist was arrested and taken and handed over to Springfield Road R.U.C station. One less to worry about.

We all piled into the land rovers and made good with our getaway too, another few minutes and all hell would have broken loose.

Start of a Riot. [kids first] Aug 12th 1979.

We had a few fatalities………………………………….taking cover where possible and returning with rubber bullets.

Another typical riot scene. Above.

INTERLUDE.1 John V. 2017?.

It has taken me a hell of a time to write this from the start, some two years ago now, and have been off it for a month or so now, but I have gained inspiration not only from the missus but also with the story that follows I am really privileged to still be around, read on…

It is Wednesday the fifth of October, I have been hospital today as my back is hurting bad at the base of my spine. It has been gradually worsening as I get older, I was diagnosed it in nineteen ninety or some time close to that year, I was told that besides me having a Hemi-Vertebrae, a curved spine, I also have a crumbling mess at the base. Epidural or man-up I was just told. I will opt for the latter. Also, on this day I was reading a post on Facebook for a John V, one of our own band of brothers, his funeral will be in Aldershot at the end of the month. I had only just got back in touch with John after Forty years and was so looking forward to seeing him again! But alas it was not meant to be, however J.V deserves a mention of note here as not only was he a great Pompadour but also a true gentleman. I recall in the early days John issuing me with a travel warrant or two to come on leave, I am sure between him, Nigel H, Don H and Nigel B they kept the Battalion going with reams of paperwork.

Anyway, it got me to thinking that my minor back problem pales in to insignificance in comparison to other people's problems, at least I am still going so RIP John and all other Pompadours who are no longer with us. Great guys one and all…444sss.

So, get on with it Smudge and stop whinging, mind you I did know that backpack with the Mortar barrel was too much for my skinny little legs. Now back to the memoirs.

Ready to go. Daily attire, strap is for riot gun.

Dropped off by Pig. Note patrol in background.

Time for a brew, N.I style.

This was relentless, day in and day out, we were lucky that we have good old Palace Barracks to go to after one of our stints, in the " Murph", the lads stationed there on four-month tours did not. Before my next story I must write about the day we lost one of our lads, but not to the evils from outside the camp gates, but from within.

Of course, you keep training and keep fit, and keep the mind active or you will lose your sanity. One day we were on the assault course with the twelve-foot log, or telegraph pole almost, there was a knack to being able to get over the assault course with one of these things. We had all done it in our basic training and it was good fitness training to carry that tradition on within the Battalion, On this particular- day though, it all went horribly wrong, we were tackling the twelve-foot wall towards the end of the course, and it was released too early and hit one of the guys on the other side, his name was Paul "Fossy" F. He took the full force of this and unfortunately died almost instantly, the paramedic was on the spot in seconds but unfortunately it was not meant to be,a great guy and fellow Pompadour, he was remembered by the new assault course trophy, The Foster Trophy. He never had the chance to take on the I.R.A.

Back to the street once more, the daily grind continues, you wonder will you make it through the day, must keep moving, take cover every time you stop, and keep alert, all the time, the bastards are not getting me, not today. I guess some of the lads had lucky charms or such items to keep them alive, I asked God to keep me alive Please, after a while though, I realised, not up to him, if there even is such a thing, it is down to me, do as I was trained, think, look, listen and all will be good. Only another six or seven months to survive. Feel sorry for yourself when you "r.t.b", not out here, feeling like that will get you killed. You have a responsibility to your "brick" we need each other. We will survive. Let us Get out there do the job over and over and over again…

We had been out here for some time and dates escape me, but word was out we were to cover a REME convoys on their way to bases in bad areas in the South of Ireland.Armagh.

So instead of the normal street patrols and F.I.B.U.A, we were going back to the nitty gritty that we all loved, Camouflage and concealment, full equipment, camouflage cream, back to the sticks. It was great to get respite from the streets, and it came at exactly the right time, we were all getting a little downhearted.

Bob Macdonald trained us hard for a couple of weeks, and we needed it, if you switch off from it, it is easy to forget the basics. Everyone in the camp looked on amazed as we ran past with full kit, cam cream, tin lids the whole works. On the last day of re- training we finished just outside the Plastic pub. [Oh the memories] and Bob Mac turned to as all and said you "spunking "lot are ready…Last man inside buys the first round!!!

We were deployed I think close to the South Armagh border or bandit country as it was known. The I.R.A patrolled like the British Army only with AK47, M16's RPG'S and balaclavas. Had we bumped into any on route they would have been screwed.

We finally reached our position late, we could just see the road the vehicles would use in the distance, and started to dig in, not good the ground was rock solid, so we dug in as best we could, just a couple of feet I recollect. We fortified the position as per "S.O.P's" with trip flares and claymores and got sentries posted. Had done my stag [sentry for two hours] and then bedded down.

Me and Smudge nine zero shared our position we camouflaged it best we could and the whole unit settled down in perfect silence.

All hell broke loose at about three thirty hours, trip flares went off and lit up the night sky, which they are supposed to do, I have never moved so fast in my life or even for my life? We were both from fast asleep out of our doss bags rifles cocked in firing position in about six seconds flat, heart pounding. We covered our arc of fire and I shit you not if anything moved it would be chewing on a minimum of twenty, 7.62mm rounds. The flares dimmed and then just the black sky and silence, then a few voices from the guys who investigated Stand down was the word. Apparently, a cow had set off the trip flare. Safety catch on. We were relieved but also on edge as our position was compromised, however we had to stay put to cover the convoy. We did so with success. Day break and we bugged out and patrolled back to the R.V.

Anyway, Smudge 90 and me both reckon that seven to ten seconds from doss bag to firing position is shit hot! Another real-life experience but carried out by some of the best soldiers ever.

IRA Patrol.

Well that was fantastic but short lived so now back to the streets and back to the "Murph", a complete shit hole crawling with the rotten terrorist bastards.

On another occasion, we were doing our regular patrolling am sure it was close to "internment" that is a person arrested can be held for forty - eight hours without being charged, this is "celebrated" every year with bombs, hijacking, shooting practice and burning of vehicles in general. Basically, it is a free for all for the I.R.A. and of course they use this to entice any patrol in to a danger zone where they would be ambushed or blown up. We all needed to be on top of our game, although always on edge, it was more prominent in this situation. We had just finished our patrol and heading back into camp when the shots fired, just went over our heads by a foot or so,, you never forget the "crack" and "thump" when it gets that close! A very distinctive sound, we were sure it was probably a AK47 or even an Armalite - M16 rifle. One of the lads thought he had spotted the area where the shots came from.

Anyway, we were zig zagging into camp, but wanted to go back out and chase down the gunman, adrenaline rushing, and wanting to catch the bastard we re-grouped, re-loaded and just about to go back out when an officer from the battalion taking over said to C/SGT Bob Mac" no don't bother Colour let them calm down a little". I think Bob Macs reply was something like" you are taking the piss Sir!! However, an officer gave the order, so we could not go, disappointed is a fucking understatement.

Anyway, we certainly earned our pay out there, and am sure most would agree we enjoyed the challenge, however not being able to shoot back is a kick in the nether regions. Very rare to get a shot at one of these especially in the open.

To lose one of your own and do nothing about it is also a sore point, especially when they singled out an unmarked escort, this is when we used to escort workers from Hospitals and would use an unmarked vehicle, would wear civvies and carry the Browning 9mm pistol for protection.

The I.R.A were not stupid and sometimes you stood out like a sore thumb, on one occasion on October 8th 1980, Paul W and L/CPL Nobby C were ambushed on the Falls Rd/Whiterock Rd junction. Five balaclava clad gunman jumped out as the vehicle was turning and fired directly into the car, Paul was murdered instantly, shot in the head, but the other guy returned fire and although shot I think four times he managed to run towards the camp and once the sentry realised what was happening, they also returned fire. We all got a little more aggressive after hearing the news about this one but couldn't do shit about it. Thankfully, Malcolm made a full recovery, but Paul did not, R.I.P Paul, duty done, remembered always, especially on Remembrance Day.

On another occasion in Ireland, we were carrying out a vehicle check point, this is where two land rovers block the road on opposite sides, so as to form a "slow area" where the vehicles have to pass through, once stopped, the people in the vehicles are "P checked", the vehicle is searched and then moved along.

We had set up the VCP and my position was at the front of the second land-rover, suddenly, a yellow Mark three Ford Cortina drove at us at some speed, it was obvious he was not going to stop, we all dived for cover! Once I recovered, I adopted the kneeling firing position and controlled my breathing, took aim into the back window of the Cortina… I was an hairs breadth of squeezing the trigger when my vision opened up and I could see people on the street, I thought for a milli-second and if I hit the driver the car would swerve and run into the a passer-by, or even a stray round could ricochet and again hit someone near-by, I decided not to open fire. Restraint and professionalism shown again.

Did the occupants realise how close they came to be shot or killed, are they still alive today? I will never know or care, but lady-luck was certainly with them that day. They were using that vehicle as a weapon, to try and kill us, those whom it is my duty to protect, there were reports of this and soldiers sometimes did open fire. The order came down from the higher echelons that we were no longer to open fire as too many "joy-riders" were getting shot or killed. What did they expect.

There was a similar act committed late eighties, I caught it on the news one evening when an unmarked car drove into a funeral, they had taken a wrong turn, I remember they were dragged from the car and shot, bodies dumped later. Although I had left the Army then it made me physically sick. It is easy to say with hindsight but if ever I was in that situation, I would have taken out twelve of the bastards and keep the last round for myself. Thirteen rounds in a Browning 9mm magazine.

Interlude…

PTSD.

After the real deal, scared for your life, shot at, spit on, trying to stop five thousand screaming people from rioting and who would kill you in the blink of an eye. Wondering every time you set out on Patrol, if it was your turn today, I found this was the right moment to mention this.

A topical subject which affects plenty of military people today is Post Traumatic Stress Disorder, a recent discovery I suppose. I know of a few members of our own Battalion who still suffers to this day, forty years after the event, no names required.

To be honest I think we all have it but all deal with it in different ways, mood swings, feeling depressed, worthless, anger, nightmares etc.

Only if you have been there and done that will anyone know how it feels, and unfortunately some suffer to the point of suicide.

I would imagine it is a hard cross to bear.

Finally, on this subject, to all the sufferers, keep strong and never give up!

Back to N.I….

This tour has seen the Battalion form closer together, we had to depend on each other for our lives! And built up stronger bonds between each unit, be it Section, Platoon or Company. We worked hard in all weather, and difficult circumstances and came out of it with success.

We all had self- discipline, respect and the honour of not letting down your mates, the Battalion, the Regiment and our Country. Most of us come out the other side intact, but some are not so lucky. Some still suffer today through PTSD.

We lost a few great Pompadours here, and they will <u>NEVER</u> be forgotten, and personally, I truly believe we did some good, against terrible situations, we were professional and carried out any given task by the book and to the best of our ability.

Peace in N Ireland 1990,s, I/we rest our case.

Ireland Promotion.

While still here in Ireland I was not expecting this...read on,

Nothing like blowing your own trumpet, but I was getting pretty good at this soldiering stuff, had been in a few years now too, mostly kept my head down and done as I was told. Was into my fourth year and handling it well. With encouragement from mates and my Platoon Commander I was volunteered, no selected to try the PNCO cadre.

This is where you attain a little rank and earn a couple of extra shillings. A Lance Corporal is a section second in command and does hold quite a bit of responsibility. A Full Corporal being the section commander, therefore I need to learn what he knows and able to take over the section if required. In a live operation or peacetime. For instance, the section commander may be away for some time and hands the reigns over to me. Daunting believe me, not so bad in peacetime if your dossing around camp but in the field a very different ball game, however I was ready for it and really wanted to show the knowledge I had accumulated.

As it happened the cadre was run by my Platoon Commander C/SGT Mac, one hell of a great leader and well respected, I knew this was not going to be easy!

To explain a little more, this is like going back to basic training, obviously we all had to take our turn as commander but also of course we were back to private soldiers so that everyone may be assessed.

This course included everything;

1. <u>Weapon Training</u>, teaching lessons on SLR/GPMG/Browning nine millimetre, a class of about twenty each time. You need to know the subject. [knowledge]. Question and Answer sessions.

2. <u>Drill/Discipline</u>. Controlling a squad of soldiers to get around in an orderly manner. Dress code, cleanliness, correctly turned out at- all- times.

3. <u>Tactics</u>. Patrol techniques, different types of patrol, crossing open ground, covering fire, camouflage and concealment, survival. How to give a set of orders for a mission, map reading. controlling your section. Decision making. Flanking manoeuvres. Fire and manoeuvre. this is just a selected few…

4. <u>Man management</u>. Looking after your section, health, how to keep warm, sleep deprivation. Eating, energy, adapting. Buddy system. Break the boredom keep switched on.

5. Military etiquette.

Anyway, the course was hard as we all expected, especially the final exercise, but came out the other side of it with a pass, but not just a pass I actually was given first place! Closely followed by my mate Ian C. We were sure that it was close, and I honestly thought I had made top five. [No Ian it was not because my Platoon Commander ran the course. [I was just better.]

I must also mention the instructors who pushed us really - hard but were always on hand to assist, without these guys we never would have made it. They helped us every step of the way and were always approachable, probably after a "Fuck Off Smudge" you should know that!   I may be a little-rusty fellas but, Geordie C, Steve D, Phil P, Bob Mac course commander, Thanks to you all, most of the names on the course I will not know and definitely -cannot remember. Quite a few passed and not many failed. One I do recall is Ian, sorry Ian C, someone had to come second!

My final word on gaining my first "stripe" is that it is really- hard to get on the ladder but so easy to lose it and drop down a rung, so standards can never drop.

The immense pride I have for achieving this lowly rank will stay with me for life, you - squaddies out there will understand, but the rest of you, will have to believe me, I cannot compare it to anything in civvy street. Nothing comes close. I suppose if you were promoted from a shop floor worker to supervisor would come close but not the responsibility.

Lance Corporal Smith.   Now that I like!

My final chapter on the Northern Ireland story rumbles on to this day, and not in a good way, to bring you up to date, recently there has been a spate of prosecutions against ex serving soldiers who had served in Northern Ireland.

Now before I go on, to bring the peace in the province there was the so called " Good- Friday agreement" included in this agreement is stated that ex members of the terrorist organisation cannot be prosecuted for past offences, in fact not only that but most were given a " get out of jail free card!" which kept them immune from prosecution and indeed actually released from prison.

Surely then it is wrong to then try and bring about prosecutions of soldiers in the same situation? It seems not, now these are on-going but it is about time that the very government that sent us there to serve and protect give us the same immunity as the terrorists themselves.

This extract was discovered on Facebook recently, I apologise for the guy that wrote it as I did not get his name but puts the point across, Please read on..

Northern Ireland was a tragedy, a cock up, and brutal for all those involved. The Civilian police could not cope with the situation, so the British Government sent in the troops. Troops who were trained to shoot and kill the enemy in event of war. They were sent in with little or no training of urban peace keeping or acting as a civilian police force.

We were tossed in to this utter political mess and social bucket of shit with not a clue. However the Officers and NCO,s had to make it up as they went along. A Big learning curve for all, to say the least.

Yes, the government came up with the "Yellow Card" to cover their arse but the soldiers on the ground had milli -seconds to make life saving, or indeed life ending decisions. Mistakes were obviously going to be made, after all the place was in a state of chaos, rule and law had broken down. Facing an enemy that hid behind women and children, would booby trap lampposts so that patrolling soldiers were blown up on passing, or cause a riot, and draw the soldiers in, before opening fire with petrol bombs and AK47,s, who could shoot at you from any window or doorway in the whole estate and then just disappear. Do we return fire at the risk of a deflected round hitting a passer- by or as we did, in almost every contact, was hold back and try to follow up as best we could. Probably find the spent cases, but the terrorist was long gone. They had no rules, or yellow card to restrain them.

The Army were tasked with taking control, defeating a hidden style terrorist enemy on both sides, a very difficult and dangerous situation.

Now is the time for the Government to put a stop to this, if there is to be no prosecutions of the terrorists with there get out of jail free card then there should also be NO more prosecutions of British soldiers.

When I awoke every morning, to head out into the streets of the Ballymurphy, scared for my own life, I did not say "right, I am going to kill somebody today". We were doing our job for fuck sake.

The government should put their hands in their pockets and pay compensation to all families, including the "bad side" for those that lost loved ones and then draw a line under the whole mess. They should say Yes, we put them there to do a job and they done it. Now let us move on.

From a military perspective, we learned the hard way, but have skills and knowledge to now deal with such a situation if it was, God forbid, ever needed again. The blood of veterans that served in Northern Ireland are now the foundations of modern strategies.

Well we finally made it through and really could not wait to get back to England, we were off to Colchester. Home.

The Old camp gates.

COLCHESTER 1979-1980.

One of, if not the biggest garrison town in the country, and a truly great place for our Battalion at this point. We travelled to several different postings from here, the dates will only be a rough guide.

Colchester had everything a soldier could want for, back in the eighties, pubs, clubs the town for shopping, all of the amenities you would need, snooker rooms, gymnasium, boxing ring for sparring, sports fields, and most of it was in the confines of the camp area. I was in married quarters in Colchester, had a nice flat a mile or so from our camp, which was Meeanie Barracks. Close to the Town Centre.

I do believe quite a few of the old Pompadours still live there to this day. Also, to me, back in the eighties, it was home and wished I had stayed there, loved every minute of it, well almost all of it. Having said that, going back recently I could not live there now too over populated for me.

The first thing we had to contend with, at Bulford I believe, was the visit of the Queen mother! This took weeks of marching practise, preparation of best dress and seemed to go on forever. We were seasoned veterans now it did not take long for us to look immaculate on the day, let me tell you there is no finer sight than the British Army in full flow at performing drill. One for the old sweats, from the present arms to the shoulder is the best drill movement ever! And when carried out correctly looks fantastic.

Anyway, time rolled on and come the big day of the parade we were ready. It must have taken about ten minutes then the heavens- opened and it started to rain. It just got worse and worse and we were all drenched! Not one crease was left in our well prepared and immaculate number two dress, our best boots were ruined, we waited almost two hours for the Queen Mum to arrive, I believe she arrived in a golf buggy type vehicle and proceeded to drive along the front rank. I cannot remember if she even got out? The trick to standing for so long in the same position is helped by slowly rolling forward on the balls of your feet and tensing your leg muscles. We also got away with a bit of chat through gritted teeth. When you see the guys pass out at these parades, it is because they do not move enough to keep the blood circulating, and consequently down you go! Well we were drowned rats that day for sure. A great piss up after though. Yes, nobody came up from home this time but did have a fantastic day.

Colchester was a great posting for us at the time, we certainly earned it from the Ireland tour.

Not sure of the order but I think it was Belize next for us, out in the jungle, so another set of skills for us to learn! Loved every minute of it, I just remember the humidity hitting you as soon as you stepped of the plane.

Not a hundred percent sure but this was about the time of the Falklands and we thought we were going for sure. Everyone was really positive, and we all wanted it so much, well I know I did. Am still disappointed that we did not make it there we, I/we were so ready for the Falklands, Instead and I am sure at the last minute, the news came that we were off to Belize instead, disappointed but hey a new challenge.

Another achievement for me in Colchester is where I learned to drive. This was done by three or four of us in a land-rover, with an instructor, constantly roaming the streets of the town on- a- daily basis, however, a good squaddie cannot perform without breakfast, so that was always the first stop!. A little café just outside of town towards Marks Tey. The driving was relentless, day and sometimes night, but would,nt you know it, passed first time! With a proper 3-point turn included, in fact I hit the kerb doing that, and thought I had failed anyway, so just carried on. The examiner, a Sgt Major said not a bad drive at all, but do not be turning into a boy racer, start with a small engine car and work your way up. I was chuffed to NAAFI breaks to have passed, could not wait to get my first car. A Volvo 340.

While in Colchester I had been told by Kev B I would make a good boxer, well ok then, why not give it a go. Let me tell you what great sport I think boxing is, I enjoyed learning the art of boxing and for a late starter in the boxing game, I achieved more than I imagined. If any of you reading this have boxed, you know what I mean, the training hurts and the fitness is immense to say the least, I was hooked from the start. I was dedicated from the start and gave it my all, in the Army there are inter-company bouts, and I started there, I learned from some fantastic boxers, but Winston B taught me from the beginning, we spent months in the old gym in Colchester, almost every day. In the Army, they expect you to train eight hours a day, every day, not possible, you just get stale and disinterested with boxing, if you change the routine daily and do not over- do the training it works better.

Not only did I box for the Battalion, we also boxed for Colchester ABC, whose Gym we used to use most weeks, I remember our trainer CPL Dave N was a great motivator, but also a hard task master, he made us train hard, but he made it enjoyable almost, and was a great trainer. Every one of the team would learn from each other, and of course some had experience before joining the Army, so they had good boxing knowledge. We had some great boxers in our team, yes in the Army, boxing is a team sport not an individual one. However, when you step in that ring, you are very much alone, my first fight was a step into the unknown but again, through experience, I reached a higher standard. You only get that from dedication and hard work in the gym. As I learned, I got better, more confident and to be honest, boxing changes your outlook, your attitude, and the way you treat people in my own personal- opinion. You need to control your aggression in the ring, if you lose your temper, you will lose, it is certainly a good life- learning curve, well it was for me. It also, in my opinion bought out the best in me and changed me to a more confident person.

I had some great fights, in the Army the team consists of 9 bouts at different weight categories from, Featherweight through to Heavyweight, cannot remember them all, but think it was feather, bantam, light, welter, light- welter middleweight, light heavy, and Heavyweight. And a couple of in-between weights I cannot remember.

One of my stand-out achievements was that the Battalion had made it through to the Semi-finals of the Army Boxing Cup, we were to fight at Chelsea Barracks against a team of The Scots Guards, this was not long after the terrible bomb placed by the I.R.A, killing horses and soldiers. The Semi went ahead, I was up against this Guardsman, he must have been seven foot tall, holy shit, I thought, how do I go about this one, well as my old trainer Dave will tell you, "slip a punch and get in close" which is exactly what I done through most of the fight, and won comfortably on a points decision. This is when I was at my best in boxing, still love the sport and it is only recently I have had to cut it down due to my back problem, still like to work the punch bag at least once a week, if I am still able to though!

Yes, great days when boxing and it is true, the Army love a sportsman and they will provide you the equipment if you want to carry on the sport representing the Army or even yourself.

The bad news is that, because I dedicated my time to Boxing, my military career stalled and suffered, and I was left behind on moving up the ranks. My own decision, no regrets. But it cost me personally, as for all these years, I was the full time, professional soldier and I let it slip. We were in the boxing team but for about 5 months of the year. Instead of learning to be a better soldier to move up to section commander and get my Corporal rank, I instead was dedicated to boxing and any spare time was spent on fitness, but bloody hell I was fit!

1982 versus Scots Guards Army Cup-semi-final [Chelsea Barracks] Battalion lost 5-4 I won my fight though, the seven- foot- tall guardsman! pictured left.

We used to run at least ten miles around the Colchester area every morning, and this was just for the warm -up, then into the gymnasium for circuit training for at least two hours, I have- to applaud our trainer Dave. N, he varied the circuits almost every session, so as none of us were bored with the same routine. As I stated previously, if you do the same thing, it is boring, and you lose interest, not good. We would then head down to the running track and continue with sprint sessions, this running and sprinting is for the leg-work, to keep the legs strong, even those of us with not too much meat on the leg, and believe me, it worked. So, the running part of training is most important. I know that three, three- minute rounds do not seem a long time, believe me when I tell you that when you are in the ring, it most certainly is. You need that strength in your legs.

Colchester ABC or Gt Dunmow 80,s [not sure?].

Usually, after the sprint sessions, it is back to the gym for bag-work and learning the art of boxing, by using the bags, shadow boxing, skipping, one to one training, we used to learn from the more experienced boxers in our group. And, of course, sparring. I used to love the sparring, as we would start sparring firstly, with the lowest weight class and then move up to the heavyweights. After completing a one -minute round with each boxer, you certainly needed some time-out. Starting with the lower weights I had to be fast and sharp because these guys were as quick to the punch, as I was, but once you spar with the bigger guys, it is great because you do not have to pull your punches and you can hit hard, a great work out. We certainly gave it our all, and once you step in to that ring, you are all alone, but the mindset is to work the other guy out, out manoeuvre him, once you decide to throw a combination of punches, throw them, or it is too late. I think I am right in describing boxing as a chess game, in the ring. Which move to make and when to make it. I certainly enjoyed my boxing days and not only within the Battalion, but also when we boxed for Colchester ABC, as we used and trained with the civilian club quite often. We used to attend civilian bouts and would get matched with a boxer of the same level and make fights that way, good experience and as always, practise makes perfect.

I fought at Featherweight, which I believe was Eight stone and thirteen three quarter pounds, not sure if that is correct, however, sometimes I would struggle to make the weight for the official weigh in, so would head off to the Embassy Club in Colchester, for the sauna, I would be sat there, eight stone, dripping wet, next to some big fat business man, he looked at me as if to say, " why would you be wanting to lose weight!", needs must, if I didn't make the weight then no fight. On another occasion, again, I struggled to lose the last couple of pounds, this time though, I would, actually, any of us that needed to shed a couple of pounds, would put on one layer of clothing, then, make a top and bottoms from black bag- bin liners, add another couple of layers, go into the shower room, turn the heat to maximum and skip or shadow box off the remaining fat! Bloody -hard work, believe me.

Inter-Company boxing, I believe I won this one too! Me on the right.

I would encourage anyone to try Boxing, it is a great way to keep fit and an individual sport in most cases, and as a team sport it is also good, you have team mates to cheer you on and you train and learn together, learning from each other. Perfect sport for the Army. I still enjoy even watching the boxing on tv and of course try to keep up with the big fights. And as I already stated, still try to work out with the bag and keep at least a little of my fitness, even at almost sixty years of age. My dream job would have been to set-up and run a little boxing club in my local area, but alas, was not meant to be. I think a two of the lads from our old Battalion team did just that, set up and run a club in Colchester. Well done to them.

I was married while stationed here, we lived in a flat in married quarters about a mile or so from camp. Ebony Close if I remember correctly, went back here a few years ago, I was in the area doing deliveries and had a forty -five break due so headed to where I can remember it was roughly. Got straight to it pretty much, pulled up and was chatting to a local resident[Squaddies Wife] and were talking about the time we were there. They were the days for sure!

Anyway, I was heading in to camp all dressed for the day, barrack dress, I think? There was a stretch that was quite open and this civvie bus drove past and soaked me from head to foot as it was chucking it down, I swear if I had caught up with the driver, I would have gave him a quick combination of wallops to the head! Still had managed to make it on parade on time and dry, you just got on with it because it meant smoothing, out here in civvie street in does not mean that much.

Yes, doing our job in Colchester, loved every minute of it. Cannot wait to get back there in May for the re-union, will deal with re unions later.

The routine at Colchester carried on, daily training schedules, a different subject to deal with, remembering all operational procedures, cleaning of weapons and equipment, guard duties, more refresher lessons on the things we have not done for some time. We also had our free time to enjoy, at the week end especially, but no one day was ever the same. Then along came our next posting, this was to Kenya.

KENYA 1980.

Are you for real! Kenya, Africa, I had to pinch myself, can you imagine, back in the 1980,s the only people that could afford to go to Africa on holiday were either rich or celebrities. Now you could probably jump on Easy-jet for thirty quid.

I also think it was one of those exchanges, we came over here and some of the Kenyan Army went over to the U.K.

Anyway, here we are stationed on the outskirts of Mombassa, actually, if I recall it was one of those Giant marquees that the Army have can sleep a whole company in one of those. A massive marquee with electric lighting running through, I remember one of the lads, ginger haired, of course, as white as a sheet, got burnt badly on the shoulders and as they were erecting the cables and wiring up the place one of the cables, must have been a good two inches thick, fell onto his blisters on his shoulders, he let out a screech of some description! The blister just popped and the slime from it spurted out in all directions. Thankfully we have our medics with us so soon had him patched up and ready for action again. But a painful introduction to being careful in the sun!

We were all taught the effects of sunburn, and more so how to avoid it happening, however felt sorry for the fair skinned guys whom had to be extra aware. And there was always going to be some that got caught out, I did on one occasion!, and learnt my lesson. I remember having to do a run with full kit and the "yoke" part of the webbing was rubbing badly on my sun burnt shoulders.

When you are carrying sixty pounds worth of kit on your back in forty degree heat there is nothing worse than to have the "yoke"[shoulder straps] digging into sun burnt shoulders, that was painful, it was real sore! Definitely controlled sun tan sessions from now on.

If you do happen to get sunburn the Army treat it as a self-inflicted wound, you were taught, and you did not learn. Deal with it and "soldier on"..

After a few weeks your body adapts and acclimatises to the heat and before long... any spare time is spent topping up the tan, controlled of course, do not lay out there between twelve midday for sure, I mean who wants to get back home looking as white as they did before we left.

Anyway, once settled in we all got used to the heat.

Hey, who cares this was Africa. Not a bed set -up to be honest, everything we needed was on camp and it was all rather laid back, I do believe we trained with some of the Kenyan Army, just doing the basics. Patrolling- techniques, camouflage all the normal stuff.

A couple of things stick in my mind from that tour, firstly, where our camp was situated, it was quite an open-area, we had the local kids around mainly scrounging biscuits from our ration packs, begging for dollars. The other was that the way they lived, a mud hut basically, the picture below is much like the actual place we were situated, picture an Army Marquee in the background and that was home for the next six weeks or so. They did let us take- a -look inside, quite impressive, and we imagined they would keep warm at night and out of the sun during the day.

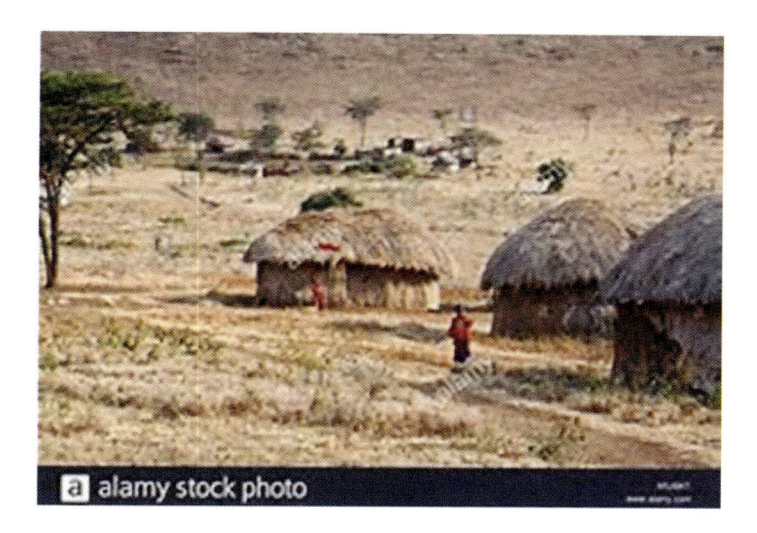

The Stores were a few hundred yards away near a small rocky area, bad idea, the local Baboon population would come around the front to get our attention, meanwhile several others would be at the back raiding our stores, very clever, stealing everything in sight. To solve the problem, we had to do "stags" and sentries around the clock to keep watch and ward off the intruders. We had all seen the funny side of their game, mind you some of those big baboons would rip your arm off! So, we did not get too close.

Watching us.

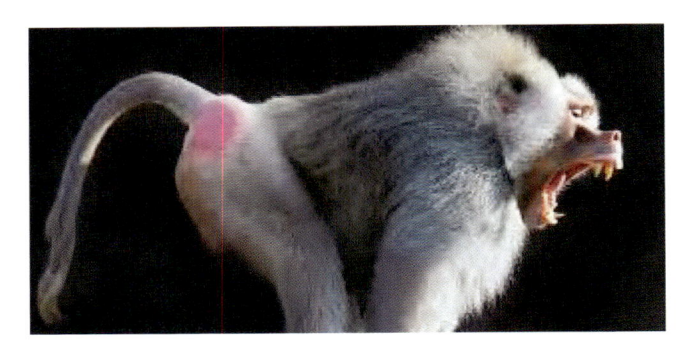

Can turn nasty.

Secondly, the place was amazing, the scenery, the animals and the people.

We played football with the local "Massai" warriors, some game, they played in their bare feet!

They also used to jump especially high, as if in a trance-like state, fantastic to watch.

I also remember visiting the Equator, and buying my Mother two carvings of MASSAI Warriors, in fact every country I was posted to, I had brought her a doll in the National costume. Never knew what happened to them when she passed away in the late nineties, possibly one of my two sisters may have acquired them.

Massai Warriors Jumping.

Local Village.

Imagine seeing this for real, unheard of back in the 1980,s.

I also recall a trip out to the Equator, I believe most of us had a picture taken there, just to prove you actually stood there, Yes, a truly amazing place to visit and will stick in my mind forever.

Mum always had the warriors on display, and anytime myself or my brother Richard would come home on leave, she would always feed and water us just as she had done when we were kids. We used to take her out for nights out down the local pubs in Kettering. Had a cracking night once, when me and a couple of the lads came on leave, had a heavy party week -end and stayed for a couple of nights. Then we moved up to Leicester for the next session, Great times. My step-Father Brian also enjoyed it. As previously mentioned, "Mum" done the best for us, and brought us up as best she could, we used to love to spoil her when we came home.

RE – UNIONS. 2014.

As I mentioned earlier our reunions are fantastic, meet the friends and comrades you have not seen in a long -long time.

This all came about because I wanted replacement medals, I had lost. My current partner and she will love this, my common law wife, had got me my medals for Christmas and it started the whole ball rolling. She was amazed on ordering that they had my name rank and serial number on record so could easily verify me as a Veteran. She amazing to be honest and as excited as myself I reckon, also I must include Lottie, she helped with it all too.

I was over the moon to receive them from her on Christmas Day.2012.

With new found knowledge we got onto the re- union site and booked up for Norwich, also we had got onto Facebook and found all we needed to really. It was good for me at this point as was fed up with the same old crap day in and day out. Yep the girls really made me happy and I have never thanked them for it, so thank you Ladies x x , but I was so grateful for their help, if only they knew what it meant to me. It brought a lot of memories, faces, stories, life or death, comradeship and if I am honest it was a little too much for me take in, for instance on entering the said re union in Norwich, I spotted Jim Glover, as we met he said: you were my section commander when I joined the Battalion, made me very proud!!. At the end of the night, the emotion of the whole event and meeting again with friends and comrades after some thirty -five or forty years, had affected me emotionally, and am not ashamed to say I shed a tear, it was too much in one night. Also, when I dressed for the re union, we have a Veterans Dress code. This is light grey or even black trousers, white shirt, with Regimental Tie and dark blue suit jacket, with Royal Anglian crest, and finally topped off with our Battalion beret with cap-badge.[Medals on some occasions]. So I had a dress rehearsal to make sure my gear looked good, a sort of kit inspection before the actual event,[Ha Ha], I will never forget the look on Delilah's face, she just stared at the medals and it was like she suddenly realised how much it meant to me, great memory. Thank You babe.

Veterans Dress.

At the first re-union I remembered after a couple of drinks, I needed to go to the toilet, so having grabbed the attention of Ian C, I introduced him to Delilah and said look after her for a while , I need the Loo, with that I shot off to the toilet where quite a few of us had assembled and were chatting away about the old times, must have been forty-five minutes before I returned to Delilah, but no problem, Ian had told her the story of the time he was on patrol and was blown fifty yards up the street on his backside from the force of the explosion from a nearby lamp-post that had badly injured one of our officers in Northern Ireland, He told us the only thing that bothered him is that the QM, [quartermaster] wanted to know how he was he was going to pay for his Denims which had, of course, a gaping hole in them. Thank you, Ian for re-living that one with us, Delilah was amazed.

The re unions are great for telling some old stories and such, or as we say: pull up a sand bag and I will tell you a story, a great get together with old comrades and the whole family. They just keep getting better. I must also mention the Regimental Day at Duxford, on entering there the current serving soldiers who greeted us called us all SIR, total respect to them and thanks, for respecting us, that is because they know how it is, to serve, and put your life on the line for your Country.

The next one is in Colchester this year, and will be the best yet, it is like we are going home.

Norwich re-union, our first

On to our third re union shortly and going "home" to Colchester for this one. Hoping to meet up with a few more comrades from the Battalion! The more I get involved the more I can remember and starting to put a few more names to all of the faces.

Colchester re-union has been and gone and again another great time was had by all, I must say from a personal point of view that I loved "Colly" when we were stationed there, I must say I did not like it at all, too over-crowded for my liking and the High Street was just a stream of people heading in all directions, not how I remembered at all, however I know that several from our Battalion have made it their home, so who am I to judge. To be honest our old barracks have all been demolished now, with only a part of the main gate fence is left standing, so our old "home" as gone. However, I did find the time to visit the Army married Quarters at Ebony Close, one of the locals told me that some of the estate is still owned by the M.O.D but most have now been sold privately. At one time I could see myself going "home" to Colchester, alas no more. I guess I have become used to the quite life.

Yes, another good re-union and it was good to see the old place, it has changed so much though.

BELIZE.1982.

Absolutely loved the place hot humid and great for fitness, we were never off the five a side football pitch morning noon and night. I was well into my fitness regime here and is perfect for you as you never stop sweating. One of my favourite postings for sure.

The first day and I remember stepping off the plane and the humidity hit us, after five minutes we were all sweating profusely. We had been to Cyprus and it was a warm breeze compared to this place. Humidity very high, not too sure on the camps there, Rideau was one of them and I think the main camp for the duration, but I have fond memories of Tree Tops, which was a camp/observation point built right on the top of a plateau and overlooked the Belize, Guatemalan border, perfect for watching the "enemy".

Rideau Camp.

The good old R.AF would drop us off at the Treetops site by Wessex Helicopter, and it was a fantastic ride, the getting there was an easy landing, however on the way out the pilot would clear the edge of the plateau and suddenly dive nose first into the jungle, a fantastic rush believe me. You have got to admire those pilots, all great guys. We used to stand on the roof four abreast at Treetops and mark the pilots landing skills , displaying boards , as if in a competition, six out of ten, nine out of ten etc, the pilots would just give us the one fingered salute back!

Sun bathing at Rideau. Quality Accomadation.

I must say that Treetops was/is one of my favourite places, dropped off if I recollect for one possibly two weeks at a time, carried out jungle patrols and observing all the time. We also had to keep the camp in reasonable state and I remember once we had to refill and replace a sandbag wall. A pain in the arse job however we got on with it as usual. While digging another shovel full of dirt as I looked a small but colourful bootlace sized snake stuck is head out of the dirt to have a go at me, I duly splatted it and chopped it in half with my trusty shovel, on showing one of the locals we were told if it bit me I would have had about five minutes to live! I think it was called a coral snake and just like the one in the picture here one of the most venomous in Belize!

Coral snake.

On the other side of the scale , we were doing a regular jungle/border patrol and as we passed under a tree one of my patrol stopped me and pointed out to me that wrapped around the branch of a tree we had just passed under as a massive snake, must have been five or six feet long and as thick as my thigh, never even seen it, scary fucking place I tell you.

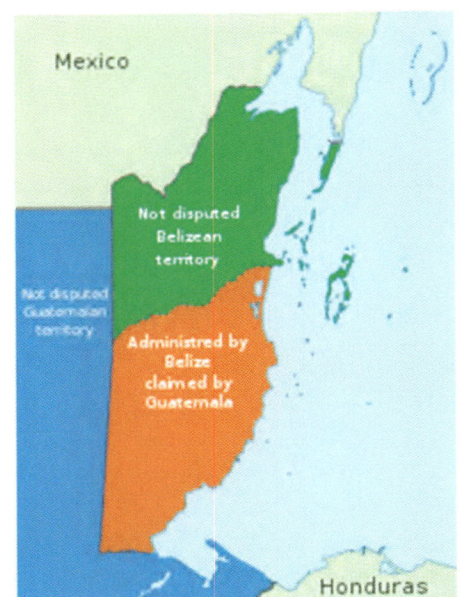

Map of Belize border.

Typical Jungle patrol.

Enjoyed the Patrolling though and learnt how to look after yourself and your unit in extreme heat conditions whilst being able to do the job. Which really was patrolling the border and peacekeeping. Unfortunately, I do not have any pictures from my time there only one or two the rest of these which were taken from another source.

I remember the patrols along the border, we would chat to the "enemy" at various points and try as best we could to communicate, we would exchange cigarettes for girly magazines and such things. Or chocolate from our ration packs for a pair of Guatemalan combat trousers I secured on one patrol. One guy took a liking to my "SLR" but he understood that no fucking way was I passing that through the fence! We got on well and we kept the softly- softly approach as it seemed to keep everyone calm. They were doing their job, just as we were.

Me on the left and Jimmy M. Belize patrol 1982?

Village deep in the jungle.

Am sure this is Simmo, making a brew!

Was sad to leave, as loved the place, so with that in mind I treated myself to a large bottle of "Blue Label Smirnoff" to take back to Blighty! Not a great deal now but back then that was a pretty potent bottle of vodka.

On my way back to the accommodation, I took a time out and sat next to the five-a-side football pitch, just relaxing! Before long a couple of the guys come over, "what you got there Smudge", after about five minutes a small gathering had formed, with plastic cups and a bottle of coke, my bottle was passed around, I didn't mind what a great way to give the place a send- off. Pretty sure we were bladdered that evening. I want to know who the culprits were too.?

- On a more serious note, I have to mention that we were posted here with the Falklands War on our minds, because just before we came, we all thought we were going to the Falklands, we were ready to go believe me and were that close but at the last minute the Royal Marines were sent in our place. I since found out that the reason we did not go was because we were not anti- tank trained! [Mechanised] On a personal note, and I believe I speak for most of the lads, we wanted to go and were at our peak, and so ready for that. I will say to the Marines that went, we were there with you, every step of the way and you all done a fucking superb job! Would have loved to stand beside you fellas. Some unnecessary fatalities, but there were going to be fatalities, but on- the -whole, a great job, professionally done. The military also found out that the kit we carried was next to useless, no actually it was useless and so out-dated, so a change and modernisation was desperately required, from the boots up!

I believe the Battalion were posted there shortly after I left, so missed out on that one.

Interlude 2. Roy Holohan. 2017.,

It is yet again another sad day, 13th July 2017. We attended the funeral of Roy Holohan.

Roy " Hooligan" Holohan, 2nd man in from right.

A great shock to all of us, we lose another Pompadour completely out of the blue! at the last re union we shared a cab to the venue and Roy and his lovely wife Lynne, they were telling us how they now just going to get on with life. Roy had suffered more than most, a couple of cancer scares and kicked its butt! Also, family issues, pretty much like the most of us, I guess. But he looked so well and as you can see from the photograph in good form. We are going to miss you "Hooligan". A top man and fellow Pompadour. RIP buddy.

Above; Kev D, Bob C, Larry M and myself discussing Roy's antics.

Well we certainly gave Roy a great send off and the service was very moving, especially for the family, his elder brother gave a great speech. He will be sadly missed.

USA. 1984.

We were still based at Colchester and our next little jaunt out was to the good old US of A.

Fort Lewis is a United States military facility located 9.1 miles (14.6 km) south-southwest of Tacoma, Washington, under the jurisdiction of the United States Army Joint Base Garrison, Joint Base Lewis–McChord. It was merged with the United States Air Force's McChord Air Force Base on February 1, 2010 into a Joint Base as a result of Base Realignment and Closure Commission recommendations of 2005.

Joint Base Lewis-McChord is a training and mobilization center for all services and is the only Army power-projection base west of the Rocky Mountains. Its geographic location provides rapid access to the deep water ports of Tacoma, Olympia and Seattle for deploying equipment. Units can be deployed from McChord Field, and individuals and small groups can also use nearby Sea-Tac Airport. The strategic location of the base provides Air Force units with the ability to conduct combat and humanitarian airlift with the C-17 Globemaster III

Fort Lewis Entrance today

Deuce and a Half- Big transport that dwarfed the old Four Tonner.

Yes, another great posting, I think I am correct in saying it was one of those exchange deals, where we went over there, and a Company came over to the U.K. It was only a six week exchange I think but loved every minute, pretty much all that I can remember is the vastness of the place, how everything was so much bigger.

We were based at Fort Worth at Seattle, not sure of the name? a massive complex and layout, it was also where the film "An Officer and A Gentleman" was filmed apparently. They certainly know how to look after their troops though. The equivalent to our own NAAFI, was called the CX, and it was like a superstore even compared with today,s standards. You could buy pretty much anything there.

We trained with some of them and as I have already mentioned we shared the ranges, they were fascinated by the SMG, and the SLR, and could not believe how heavy it was compared to the M16 which we got our hands on in Belize.

I remember us all going out on the town for a few beers, they were very strict, and you had to have I.D or no drink. We were all in one bar and cannot remember who, but was quite clearly one of the "oldies" did not have I.D, however I did, they just would not serve him so I said I would have a pitcher of beer and give the kid a coke! I only looked about Fifteen. On the same night, the place we were in was a little too un-lively for our excited souls, so we decided to head off somewhere else and asked the bartender for some directions, he said yeah couple of blocks down the road and hang a left for another pub. So off we went, well after about fifteen minutes walking we were a little "naffed" off, did not realise a couple of blocks was like 2 to 3 miles!! Called a cab, I think!

I also remember having a day on the ranges, we were zeroing our weapons [S.L.R] as usual firing groups of five to ten rounds or so, then adjust sights, up or down as required and then another grouping of five to ten rounds, anyway, along came a platoon of American squaddies with their M16,s and all lined up, and emptied whatever ammo they had at a big circular target, ceased fire, slung the weapons and off they went? Peace through superior fire power, I guess! Mind you, half of them probably never hit the bloody target at all.

The Americans really liked the British Army, and to be honest we all got on with each other well, no language barrier helps, mind you they do have some words that mean exactly the wrong thing in English, for example, on one of our nights on the town one of our section asked the barmaid for a JUG of beer, "SAY WHAT"! Was the reply with a rather awkward look from the afore-mentioned barmaid, the explanation being that a Jug means a Breast in the States, so in effect he asked for a Tit of beer? No wonder he received the evil eye. The situation was sorted with the minimum of fuss. Some of the Rangers looked pretty mean to us and not good to upset our hosts. mind you, they did not want to upset us either!

The equipment and resources they had, the size of the barracks, housing accommodation, vehicles, weapons and numbers of troops even back then was mighty impressive, but despite all of that I personally thought we made the better soldier, I do believe our training was harder, stricter and more exertive and detailed than theirs. However, having left the Army before the Iraq and Gulf War all kicked off, I never had the privilege of serving alongside our greatest ally, am sure the new breed will be able to tell me, but what I can tell you is they were great to work with, were professional, hard-working, and like us, immaculately turned out. And they loved the Brits!

They also loved our weapons and I especially remember the SMG was a favourite of theirs, and one ranger wanted to swap my SMG for an M16, would have gone for it, but think the thought of trying to hand in my M16 to the armoury at the end of the day, a little too difficult to get away with! Would have been glasshouse time for sure!..I think i know now why they liked it so much, I guess it reminded them of the WW2 weapons, and to be honest it was a little dated, however in the SMG,s defence though, and as I recall, an effective and most excellent weapon used in the correct environment. Close Quarter fighting to be precise.

SMG 9MM

M16 ARMALITE USA ISSUE

USA- Downward slope.

At this point that I must mention that here in U.S.A is where I began to go downhill, A big mate of mine Titch W, a P.T.I one of the best too! Anyway, he pulled me to one side and said he had some bad news.

So, let me put this into perspective, here I am on my way doing well, loving the job and my rank, looking to move upwards, happily married, life is great what could possibly go wrong.

Well the news was that apparently as soon as we got on the plane for the States my missus had another guy round, gutted to say the least, I took it badly and of course took to the drink, was angry and could not believe it. Thanks to CSM S for allowing me a little time to gather my thoughts and let off some anger, for what I said to him he could have locked me up for a long time, I have always respected the military etiquette and lost it a little that day, Thank you again, Sir.

Anyway, without dragging it on it was doomed from that day, yes there is a familie,s officer and his staff who assist you with guidance but not for us I am afraid, how could you trust someone who would do that! This was also confirmed by my brother Richard who popped in to the flat at Colchester a few times, as he was Lorry driving in the area, one time he told me he popped in and there were bodies all over the flat, lying in the hallway, on the sofa, party time again and she was in bed with another fella. We tried to keep it together for the daughter,s sake, but did not work out.

Finally, on this matter, yes, I did have an affair with a married woman during our turbulent time, but we were already finished as a couple. That did not work out well either and I suffered for my woes, so it was all <u>MY</u> fault!?,we tried to stick it out and lasted until the early part of the posting to Germany, the end was sour when it came, emptied the house and my bank account, however I did not expect it to go on forty years after the event, where my ex was slagging off my family and trying to ruin my current relationship. Unfortunately, the daughter was also poisoned against me.

No names are required here and suffice it to say the finger was always pointed at the wrong person. Some people still around today, take note.

I am guilty of some terrible things and will take it to my grave. End of story…..

Let us move on with the military,

So, despite the upheaval in my career, I really did enjoy my time in the States and unfortunately have never been back, I must add it to my bucket list!

My career was on the downward slope and I found it difficult to keep soldiering on, but it is what I was taught, I did not want to give up, I loved my job and so regret the way it ended. If I had the chance to do it all again I would, let me tell you the Army is a fantastic place to be, but you have to live by certain rules and regulations. Sure, you can maybe bend and stretch them a little but try to cut corners or not do as you should, and you will be found out! For the moment though, despite the anger, hurt and pain that this problem had caused, I needed to get on with it and keep going.

Only recently I have found out that I actually left Recce Platoon and had gone to Mortar Platoon during my last couple of years, if it wasn't for one man I would have given up long before, so Thanks Polly I will always be in your debt my friend, I will also take this opportunity to apologise to people who believed in me and I had earned their respect and then sadly let them down, fuck it I am naming names, apologies to Monty, Brian H, Billy E, Dave N, Gap D, Titch W [bad news bearer], Maj S,CSM S, Bob Mac also all of those whom I served with, taught, knew, respected and served under me.

Despite all of this, and during this difficult time, the good always out-weighs the bad. My proudest time was before I left and screwed up at Brecon, on the Section Commanders Course, Prior to the course I needed the eexperience of my own section, so was given the rank of acting Corporal, and had my own Section, my own "lads" to look after, train, encourage, reward, keep safe and let me tell you, there is nothing better than earning respect of people with whom it was your duty to look out for, a rule that served me well was ; Never ask anyone to do anything that you could not do yourself, or have done! You have to Command respect, not Demand it!

 I will never forget the guys, my section; John Har, John M ,Roy ,Mike L, John Hew, Tony G, Paul S, forgive me fellas, cannot for the life of me remember them all.

I also remember, for the life of me no dates available, taking my Section out for the first time on exercise, where I do not know or it escapes me, but as a section we all have our given jobs to do and of course, being the New Section commander on the block, my section inevitably always ended up with the crap jobs that were needed to keep the position in running order, this means digging latrines or "shit-pits", stag duties, keeping the platoon area secure with a rotating 2 hours on duty and four hours off and other trivial minor tasks.

No problem doing this, but after a couple or three days of doing this my guys got a little aggravated and to be honest, proper pissed off, and asked why we were always doing the same menial tasks, I agreed with them and said I would sort it at the next Platoon O group. I guess that possibly Brian H, Gap D will recall, at the O group I said that my Section were a little pissed off with the same crap and so was I, I said to the Platoon Commander a second Lieutenant, Lt S give it to one of the other Sections, as my guys and of course myself were pissed off with it! Also the fact that myself and my Section also needed the patrolling and other special duties to be able to learn and practise our " in the field" training. So, after that day, no more Shit shovelling for my guys we done our share. They were pleased that I had spoken up for them and so was I, the other two well experienced NCO,s had also realised I was not going to be shit on anymore. Another valuable Learning curve- Stand up for yourself and your men, they will respect you for it. Was a big testing moment for me too you must understand, being the new boy on the block! But respect given to the other two NCO,s and our officer for backing me up. My wording really put the point across methinks. I think I said "my guys are not just "Shit shoveller,s" and just because I am a new section commander means we get all the piss poor jobs, so don't Fuck with me, seemed to have done the trick. I must say that every section commander and Platoon Commander did help me, there is so much to learn as a new Section Commander.

<u>Next Step</u>

Once you have attained the rank of Lance Corporal it seems the Army like to keep you learning fast, in most cases, shortly after getting that rank you will be put forward for the Section Commanders course at Brecon to attain the rank of Corporal. Bear in mind that we are now stationed in Germany, and that costs a substantial amount to send soldiers away for these courses. I suppose because you are fresh and done well then it makes sense to keep the momentum going and push you on to the next step. So, here I was, to be shipped back to Blighty to attend my next course. I never complained, why would I, and well to be honest I was good to go, as well as the responsibility that goes with the job, you also earn a little more in the wage packet. Win -win situation.

Briefly, I need to mention the Section Commanders course at Brecon, I arrived ready to go and looking forward to the challenge, I so wanted to do well, as I had done in earning my first step on the way to climbing the ranks, as most of my old mates had already achieved. For me to come first on that course was really pleasing, and I knew that I could do well here at Brecon.

Basically, all I can remember is arriving, getting settled in at the barracks, meeting everyone from the different Regiments, all chatting about our current postings and generally finding our- way around the place, the first couple of days were going well. It was going to be tough, but I was more than capable, and we all worked hard the first few days.

Then we had got to the week-end, some decided to stay in camp and revise, others shot off in the own direction, possibly head home for a last hoorah before the hard work began. I decided to stick around and check out the local pubs in town. So a small group of five or six of us headed to the town for a few well-earned beers, this was where it all started to go wrong, I cannot remember exactly what caused the argument but I was being a little loud and one of the others had told me to " shut my mouth", bad move, anyway we wanted a fight but nothing came of it, not until we had actually got back to camp, as I walked through the barrack room door he began giving abuse, like a red rag to a bull, I hit him with a combination of punches, thinking I had it sorted, he then stood up somehow and actually round-house kicked me in the head, just connecting above my eye. We were both in a bloody mess and we both agreed a truce, and that we had better get up to the Medical centre.

Funnily enough, after such a nasty fight, we actually helped each other, blood-soaked to the Med centre. We realised our error and blamed the Demon drink, and that was that…

We were a mess the next morning, and our Squad Instructor said we had to go straight to the training area, we had no time, after another visit to the Medical Centre, to get our equipment or weapons. It was my own doing, but once I mouthed off at the instructor and refused to carry on until I had my equipment, he told me to return to camp! we were doomed. Well I was anyway.

The following morning, we both had to parade at the Camp Commanders office, marched in by the RSM, we could not believe that we had both been kicked off the course! And were to return to our units, immediately.

My own C.O was not a happy man, this was the start of my decline, and I regret it to this day, if only I had stayed in camp and revised as it is what I had planned to do, is too late now and I did apologise to the C.O, I did not loose my Lance Corporal rank but did not feel very good about myself, not only had I let my own high standards slip, but let down my guys, my Battalion and all of the fantastic people whom helped me to get there in the first instance. Is only forty years late, but apologies to all.

I still feel bad about it after all this time, these things stay with you as a soldier. I hope that a comrade or two can understand what I mean, and no doubt you still also suffer now, as I do.

GERMANY BAOR.

So, it was goodbye Colchester Hello Germany, the Cold war.

This was a permanent move, so the whole Battalion had to be packed up and moved, our destination was Elizabeth Barracks Minden.

This is a brief description of our roll here.

The B.A.O.R had 4 Main elements,

a. Main Force was 1 BR Corps at Bielefeld

b. British Rear Combat Zone in Dusseldorf which was to re-supply the fighting formations.

c. British Communication Zone at Emblem, Belgium tasked to receive reinforcements from G.B and to co-ordinate onwards to BR Corps.

d. The Berlin Infantry Brigade some 3,000 strong and under control from Allied Control Council at Berlin.

Manpower was between 60-75,000 troops of BAOR commanded by a 4 star General at Rhiendalen.

The British Army of The Rhine was the main element of the British Army based in W. Germany from the end of the Second World War until 1994 it was tasked with being prepared for counter - aggressive operations by the Soviet Union and Warsaw Pact armoured forces.

At the end of World War Two the British Army was drastically reduced in manpower that the Former British Rhine Army was only 2 Divisions, the 7th Armoured Division and the 2nd Infantry Division, these were based in former Wertmacht barracks located in Lower Saxony and North Rhine Westafalia.

They were replaced by the Armoured Division in 1950 and 6Armoured Division in 1952. Forming 1 British Corp part of NATO ,Northern Army Group Nothag.

They were restructured and re-equipped with new weapons.

Although not strictly classified as an operational duty, we were the main defence of attack from the Soviet and Warsaw Pact countries at the time of deployment.

I must say another one of my favourite postings, even with the spiral downwards I really did enjoy Germany, there was plenty to do and all areas open to everyone, unfortunately I missed out on the chance to visit one of the old concentration camps, the guys that did said an unforgettable experience. Maybe one day, again, I will add it the bucket list.

I especially liked the training and the job we were there to undertake, which was basically wait for the "Red - Ruskies" to come trampling through Germany and onwards.

I loved to be in the field, loved the mud – cold – rain - ice -jungle – desert - plains -valleys, digging the 6 foot trench to live in, just basically being out-there, however, I could never understand the lads who volunteered for Norway, get real for fuck sake, I don't mind getting cold but that was stupid cold!

Please read on for Germany..

I was still married when we got to Minden and were given a very nice three bed house surrounded by Staff Sergeants and WO2,s. I had my Company commander, Major Steele to thank for that, to be honest, I was very lucky to have a good rapport with him, he very often let me off light when possibly I could have been locked up. I met up with him probably about thirty-five years later at The Swan in Market Harborough, I still addressed him as Sir! A truly great officer. Very well respected as all were. Unfortunately, I have not seen him since although I live near to Market Harborough.

I have got to be perfectly honest here, I am sure

I remember on one occasion that we had our trenches dug by the engineers, they were perfect, main fire trench and two sleeping bays, with wriggly tin walls and pickets to hold them in place, fantastic, at night as I got into my maggot [sleeping bag] I had tied a candle in a tin on the side of the trench, armed with a mug of tea and mess tin of stew, followed by A.B biscuits and a well earned ciggy! Luxury! A hell of a lot easier than digging them yourself that is for sure.

On another occasion I remember we had dug in with several houses to the rear of our position, we must have been on the edge of the training area as about 50 metres or so behind us were a row of houses. The locals came out and brought us drinks and cakes, a nice gesture we thought, mostly they tolerated us in their country, some of the older German people did not like at us at all.

Typical Mortar set up, Germany [BAOR].

Information. The total weight of Mortar Equipment [pictured above] a section carries, with 2Two Rounds, is 168 pounds, divided by a three -man crew, which equates to fifty-six pounds per man, plus his personal equipment of thirty pounds, eighty-six pounds per man total.!

To continue, the Battalion soon settled in and I finally got my wish of joining Recce Platoon, I had to keep badgering a guy named Billy Eke, Colour Sergeant and the Platoon Sergeant for Recce, I knew him quite well from the rifle companies and virtually begged him to get me in.

Am not sure which was my favourite job, rifleman/ Lance Corporal in a section, Mortar man, did a little time there too, Milan Platoon, for the briefest of time, but has got to be Recce Platoon.

To join Recce Platoon, you had to have done at least three years, minimum, this was the cream of the Battalion and just the best job! Our Scimitars took us everywhere, but the Rifle - Companies, sometimes, still had to use the good old D.M.S. and Tab into position.

In the "new" modern Army we were now mechanised, so we had the Scimitar FRV, a truly great piece of equipment for its time, I believe it served the guys well during the Falklands War too.

Rifle companies were also mechanised using the good old F432 APC.

This was a purpose- built recce vehicle, fast, light, highly -manouverable 10 tonne tracked vehicle. Armed with the 30mm Rarden cannon, a crew of three, driver, gunner commander.

Scimitar FRV. We loved it and still do.

On the move. Recce Platoon.

Once the Battalion had been called out, on the Parade square, all in their pre- arranged places, rifle companies, heavy weapons, mortars, Milan, and rear echeleon. Equipment checked, Ammunition issued, camouflage cream applied, If people were out of camp then MP,s were sent out to round them up, was it the real deal or another practice/exercise?

As Recce Platoon we were First out the Main gates, we were the forward eyes for the Battalion and would report back directly and only to the C.O. Gets the adrenalin going just to write about it now, I remember it so well.

So, it was all out training and back to basics really, equipment checks regularly, training and more training so that when the call came, we were ready to deploy.

60lbs of Kit. Kitted out for deployment.

Recce Platoon Scimitars on the firing point at Sennelager.

Live Firing. Not sure which one I am in?

So, the routine went on and we settled in again, Germany was such a clean place, you would never find a piece of litter anywhere, wonder if it is the same today? As I recall there were no run-down buildings or even scruffy cars on the road, just before we arrived they lowered the overseas living allowance although there were still Private soldiers driving around in B.M.W, cars, we sure missed out on that one, just outside of the main-gate there were a couple of Bars, shops, barbers so ideal if you did not fancy the NAAFI for a pint. Yes, all of you Pompadours, the infamous "Eckys" Bar, a great place. More on that one later. Yes, a great camp lay-out. I have never been back there either but am hoping to in the not too-distant future. I do believe that some of the older generation were not happy with us being their but on-the-whole a lovely country. Being in the military we had strict dress codes and how to present yourself in public places and that really helps when in any Foreign country. You are not allowed to bring the Regiment into disrespect by bad behaviour. I also remember that jay-walking was a no go, as it carried an on the spot fine maybe 30 DeutcshMark, pissed or not, that was a tidy sum back then. I don't know probably £50 now.

NAAFI Elizabeth Barracks. Minden.

One of the Company Blocks.

Free-time was great too, plenty of places to see, freedom to go pretty much anywhere in the country, and more to the point everything that was needed was close to or in the camp perimeter. The married quarters [pads] were virtually right outside the rear gate. I was still living out of camp for a while anyway, but inevitably the end of my pretend marriage was over. I will never forget the day I moved back to the barracks, a real sense of relief, because the last few years were not nice, I think we alternated week ends off. Almost everyone in the Battalion knew each- others business, let,s face it we were a Battalion family living in a confined area, no different than any small town in the U.K.

Moving into camp was fantastic for me at this point, I needed it, however not all rosy to start with though as I had to clean-up the married quarters because the ex-wife had already left. She cleaned the place out of everything and sold the lot to her buddies around the pads, that really didn't bother me that much but what did is the fact that she also cleaned out my bank account! I have forgotten the Families Officer,s name but a complete and utter arsehole, another one whom pointed the finger at me without first checking the facts. Scrubbed that place from top to bottom several times but was never good enough for him. Issued me with a rather large bill for nothing really. If I ever catch up with him, even now, well I will not be held responsible for my actions. There is still fight in the old dog yet. He will get a combination if I can still produce one! Finally got the prick out of the way and got on with it.

At the time, I was still into my Boxing, but the soldiering was taking a back seat, I always loved the fitness even without the boxing, still loved my football too. [see Cyprus].

This was the time it all started to go wrong and turned to the" best friend in the bottom of a glass",

Any free time now I was always in the mess or out in "Eckys" Bar sinking a few. Do not get me wrong there was a drinking culture in the Army back then, but we could all sink five or six pints and still be on parade the next day, 05.00hrs good to go.

Parade Square [recent] RSM would not be happy!!

NBC training. Mike Lawrence, Dave Petit, Lance Flower and myself. The two far left I cannot remember or even see.

On or around the 3rd of September 1984 another call- out to test us out, however this time we were actually-deployed, Yes, the beginning of Exercise Lionheart!

The Beginning.

LIONHEART comprised two interlinked exercises, FULL FLOW and SPEARPOINT, the former, a deployment through the Rear Combat Zone and the latter, the field training exercise for 1(BR) Corps.

Executed in 1984 that involved 131,565 UK personnel, regular, reserve and Territorial Army, the largest exercise since the end of WWII.

290 flights from the UK transported 32,000 personnel. This initial air movement was followed with 150 sailings across the North Sea and English Channel using civilian ferries. The sea routes carried 23,600 personnel with 14,000 vehicles and trailers.

750 Main Battle Tanks were involved and most crossings over the Rhine were conducted with combat bridging, making the assumption- that all civilian bridges had been destroyed. 1(BR) Corps were deployed with 3th and 4th Armoured Divisions and 1st Infantry Division.

The Enemy [orange forces]

Providing the opposition (Orange forces) were, 6,300 German (1 Panzer-grenadier Brigade), 3,500 Dutch (41st Armoured Brigade), 3,400 American (1st Armoured Brigade)and 165 Commonwealth (from Australia, New Zealand and Canada) personnel.

Lionheart was the first time US forces had operated in Europe with their new M1 Abrams MBT and M2 Bradley combat vehicles. The newly re-formed 5th Airborne Brigade also formed a second opposition group, joined by elements of the Life Guards and 10th Gurkha Rifles.

13,000 RAF personnel were involved, deploying Harrier and the newly introduced Tornado aircraft.

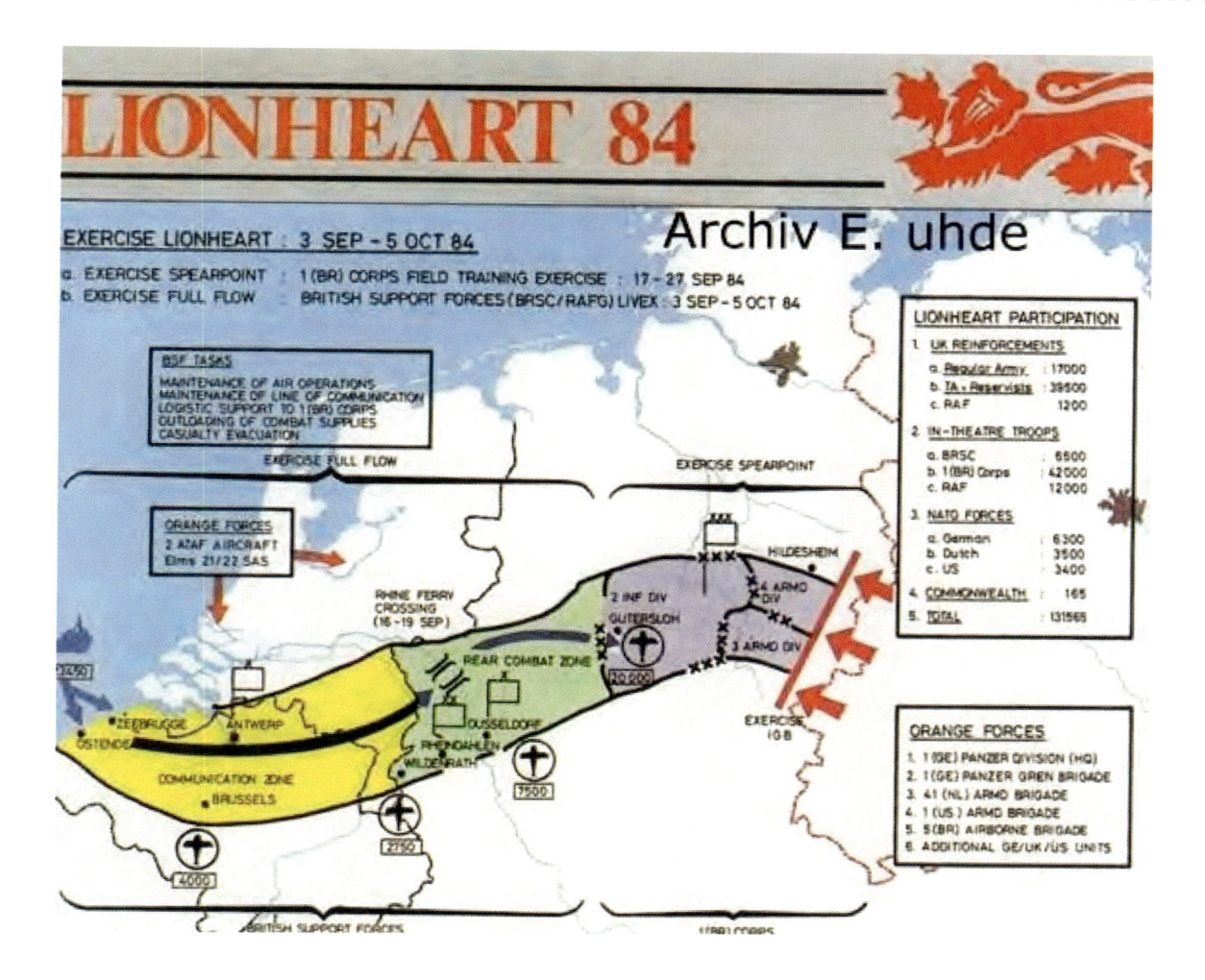

It was the first opportunity to conduct a major exercise with Challenger 1 Main Battle Tanks, Saxon and tracked Rapier. The still in early development Warrior Mechanised Infantry Combat Vehicle was also introduced.

Unfortunately, there were fatalities, 3 in total, 7 were also seriously injured but considering the amount of men and machinery that were deployed this was inevitable.

A quick note that you can still view videos on You Tube and well worth a look to see how things have changed! Here is the link to one of the first video/reports on Exercise Lionheart, copy and paste in to your browser and take- a -look back at what we accomplished.

https://youtu.be/KU-qmHYXosQ }

Although most of the footage is about the rear echelon bodies and the T.A that flew or shipped out from the U.K.

So away we go, and as I have previously mentioned being Recce Platoon, we were first out of the camp gates, this time felt different than the normal short trip out and back, the adrenaline was pumping and were really looking forward to at least showing what we could do on the battlefield under simulated conditions. Every squaddie will tell you that some exercises are the same old routine however we had to treat them all as reality because God forbid, if it was for real then you had to be ready.

With an Umpire close at hand, they wore White arm -bands so they were easily recognised, we had to do everything by the book, [Standard Operating Procedures] as we always did. We were Professional Soldiers.

All equipment was checked, vehicles checked, weapons oiled and good to go, if you had forgot something too bad, we were on our way. I will never forget the 8 Scimitars rolling out of the camp gates, [a great sight], it was raining as usual if I recall, who cares.

Incorporated into this exercise was live firing, which is something different to the usual "blank" rounds, and it also gave the whole deployment more realism, as this is how it would be, so soon after deployment we were given co-ordinates for an R.V point. This was the live firing ranges.

Let me tell you this was impressive, firstly we had the A10 Tank busters fly over and take out some of the targets [old tank hulls and assorted soft targets, land rovers and troops [Fig 11 targets].

The noise and firepower from an A10 is awesome. Our Scimitar is fitted with a 30mm Rarden Cannon and we can get quite a few rounds down quickly, however the Warthog as a 30mm Gatlin gun fitted, so a complete hail of 30mm shells all impacting the target at the same time is unstoppable. I do not think there is any Tank that could survive such an impact.

I will never forget the noise for sure.

Check it out on You Tube, it is well worth a look.

Thunderbolt A10 [Warthog] firing the 30mm Gatlin cannon.

Firing On the move...fast!

Then it was our turn to take out any left-over targets, firing and manouvering the Scimitar was fantastic, I was the driver, so getting the guys into position for targeting took some practice, the smell of cordite and the adrenaline pumping, an unforgettable experience, ok the "enemy" were not firing back at us but all the same it remains one of those "once in a lifetime" achievements fulfilled.

As we moved on to the next phase, the Company,s would all come through the live firing phase, they cleared up whatever we had missed, boots on the ground. So that all phases were practised for real, I.e Company, Section orders right down to each individual soldier. We had all done this before in training. It was their turn.

As the Rifle companies cleared up, we then moved further forward to carry out reconnaissance on the Orange forces, we would find the high ground and basically wait for the enemy to come into view. Watching and waiting.

In simulated Battle conditions we moved quickly and covered plenty of ground in the first day, at our first RV we "cammed "up and got in to the usual routine for the night, sentries out, preparation of equipment, ready to move in a second.

On to the second day and we were now approaching the Orange Forces area and were ready to be attacked, not so, again back to the night routine again.

The next morning when we were woken up by the night sentries we found ourselves in a small copse on some high ground, it was dense with foliage and plenty of trees around for cover, we were situated deep in the middle. We had got set up just before dusk, camouflage nets, sentries worked out and food and a brew, we settled for the night, a chilly night but not too bad. A perfect spot. Undulating ground, just slightly higher in the direction of the enemy threat. Open rolling hills and several more small wooded areas dotted around. Visability was good.

Open ground as described. A little more hilly than the picture suggests.

Scimitars on the move [not ours]

However, after virtually just opening our eyes the ground started shaking by the rumbling of enemy tanks as they passed by our position, we acted fast, back into vehicles, not a sound and stayed put. As the vehicles passed, we counted and using tank recognition could relay the information back, however we soon realised we were surrounded in every direction.

No panic, our commander Sgt Billy Eke was calling in to the CO with all the numbers, vehicle types, direction etc. In all of this time, say 2 hours not one of the vehicles, there must have been 40 or more heavy tanks, had seen us and I shit you not these massive Panzers were about 15 feet from our position passing by the copse, if one of them had chosen to come through the middle we were screwed.

Luckily, they did not!

Similar to the sight we had, as we careered out from the copse.

However, we could not stay in our position for much longer, in a real- life situation we probably would have tried to sneak out in the cover of darkness.

But this being a Military Exercise the umpires were asking what we were going to do, as we had given so much information back to callsign nine [our Commanding Officer] and needed an escape route.

I think I am right in saying that we were told to create as much havoc as possible and take out as many enemy tanks as possible. In other words, a suicide mission!

We made our plans, Sgt E and all vehicle commanders Steve N, Kevin M forget the other one, set us up for our final fling. Firstly, it was time to remove our cam nets and get all equipment stashed away. Then load up with ammunition [thunder flashes in our case [to simulate us firing the 20mm Cannon]. All matter of grenades, Green, Red and even yellow, some for cover and some for simulating firing and some for smoke cover.

We had split into 2 groups if I remember correctly, we charged out with all guns blazing. The Scimitar was a highly -manouverable vehicle and we used it to great effect that day.

Four vehicles one way and four the other, throwing "thunder-flashes", and smoke grenades as we hurtled along, with that the tanks lined up on top of the hill simulated firing back. Utter chaos.

When we arrived at the bottom of the hill the umpire stopped us, and we discussed the outcome.

I think he gave us three kills and we were wiped out! A little harsh we thought.

But unbeknown to us, about seventy or so men of our Battalion were at the bottom of the hill playing "dead" sitting around and having a brew.

As we were charging out from the copse, they were all cheering and shouting like crazy, we really gave them a good show.

In reality, we would never have moved, from that position, unless compromised, and if we did, we probably would have sabotaged the vehicles and left on foot to go on and recce another area causing chaos and assisting the Battalion.

It was not to be, that was us out of the exercise and now "dead" along with our other brothers in arms.

I believe I am right in saying that in a real attack, if it ever happened, the top brass figured our life expectancy in the field was six minutes! We done well to survive. A great experience but over all too quick.

I believe the MOD have issued a B.A.O.R Medal recently and was debating whether to get one, it is not a ceremonial one so cannot be worn with our others. After a while and much deliberation, the conclusion was that yes, it may not have been a "live" operation, but we were there just in case the old "Cold War" kicked off and would have been frontline if it had. So, I believe we earned that right.

In fact, the British Army are stationed all over the World in various operations, but we should not be handing out medals for any old tour or posting. We were in Germany for a reason. And once again we done our job to our usual professional standard, as always. I believe there is a new Cold War now, so good luck to the guys on that one.

This was the last Hoorah for me, from this point on I really cannot remember what went wrong, I started to give up as a soldier and I had decided it was time for me to leave the Army. I think I just lost the plot completely, the part I can remember is going on CO,s Orders and saying to him I wanted out. Especially after the Section Commanders course had gone so wrong, his response was that I was a fool, had the World at my feet, he said all of the guys I had joined with were now Sgt,s and pushing on, while I was still only a Lance Corporal. He also said if I had carried on soldiering, instead of giving it up for my Boxing, that may have helped. He finally stated that he would let me go, and gave me 21 days "nick" to seriously think about it, as he thought it was the wrong decision by me.

He was so right, I regret the decision to this day and have had to live with that.

My first few days in the Battalion Guardroom were hard, all of the Provost and Sgt L knew me and that I had served 10 years already and realised that I was super-fit and no amount of drill, running, or sit ups would bother me. After a few days they left me inside, to clean the cells or something.

One time while serving my time the Provost Sgt John L, came to my cell one day and said "Look, why don't you stay in", as a member of his Provost staff, and just sign for one more year, he would keep me on the right track, it was tempting but said no to that too. If only.

Veterans dress code.

It felt strange leaving and was hard for me to adapt to civilian life, I don't think I ever have done really. I still miss it after all this time, however I have a son called Ethan, who I think is going to follow in my footsteps and join. I taught him early, and he loved the chance to get out in the dirt. I will not discourage him, in fact I encourage him as much as possible, no matter how mad the World has become just recently. He has definitely got the Army mentality, and by the time this little book venture of mine is completed, he should be I.J.L.B Harrogate, I am relieved to hear the same routine goes on today in the new modern Army. He has a lot to look forward to.

Nice-job Ethan, starting early- where is the "cam" cream!!

Just recently via the Social media, and having found my old Pompadour family, Ethan and myself went along to our Regimental Gathering at Duxford and luckily enough the lads currently serving brought along some of the equipment. Wow! They have clothing for all weather conditions, and everything seems more compact compared to our old 58 Pattern webbing and backpack. As I remember right from the early days of training this webbing would be uncomfortable, digging in to your side, after another few miles of "tabbing" it would be rubbing somewhere else. When you had to attach the large pack/backpack to the yoke it pulled the back down and your waist belt would be pulled up to your chin! Digging in to your shoulders as well, inevitably it would slip of the padded section. Hey, we got through it though, what pain?? and the next day, and the next etc…

Here are a couple of examples of changes to Equipment and Weapons.

58 Pattern webbing.

Webbing -Today. Tailored to fit and why not.

Carl Gustav 84mm. Anti-tank.

NLAW. Anti-tank.

SLR.7.62mm. Changed in 1986.

SA80 5.56mm from1986 to present day.

However, I did notice that the new body armour is very heavy, the new recruits wear it in stages thankfully, in my day we just had the "flak" jacket in Northern Ireland, it would probably stop a 9mm round from about 30metres. Not much else.

Yes, I must say that the new modern Army is moving with the times, in the equipment department. The other pleasing thing is that just as we were trained some 40 years ago, the training is the same as it was back then, and why not, "if it aint broke don't fix it" springs to mind.

I have added to my bucket list something that I really need to do, to and that is to spend a day or two with one of the Battalions, whether it be in the U.K or at one of the overseas postings, preferably Cyprus, just to see for myself and to meet some of the men, and now women, whose duty it is to keep us safe in our beds at night. As we did some forty years before.

N. Ireland [re-visited]

Am working from the office these days, however a couple of years back, whilst still able-bodied enough to drive, a delivery came up for Ireland. I was offered the job and of course said yes, not just for the nostalgic reason, but also a change from the normal Motorway network in England also a change of scenery and I was curious.

I was fine, until I drove off the ferry, and I could see Belfast soon approaching, as I neared, the streets seemed recognisable and I knew exactly where certain events had happened some 35 years previous, I am not ashamed to say there was a tear in my eye, it was like patrolling the streets, the fear came back, and I was scared for the first time in a long time!! Goosebumps even! I soon got to-grips with it and was muttering to myself" wake up you fool it is different now, there is now peace, where once there was hatred" you are a civilian, and nobody will recognise you. I did not want to be a civilian, I wanted my protection back, the lads, the "flak jacket" my rifle. The hairs on the back of my neck were tingling, I was visibly shaking, and I had to pull over. "Get a grip of yourself Smudge" I inwardly shouted to myself, After ten or so minutes, I had calmed down and got my act together, everything was "normal" again.

Anyway, I believe it was just the initial shock of being there, so many memories, good and bad, after my delivery was done I had missed the next ferry, so had a couple of hours to spare, I drove to Holywood, home of Palace Barracks, it still used as an Army base I believe.

I felt so much better, parked up and strolled around the town I had known so well back then, as we were based there for 18 months in 1978, now I felt safe, as I recalled when some of us popped out of camp on our rest period for a beer down the local pub. Well almost safe.

Well, I made the next ferry back and had to endure another night, at least I had a room for the night in one of the motorway services, as it was too far to drive all the way back, this helped really, I needed the time to reflect.

I doubt I will be going back again..

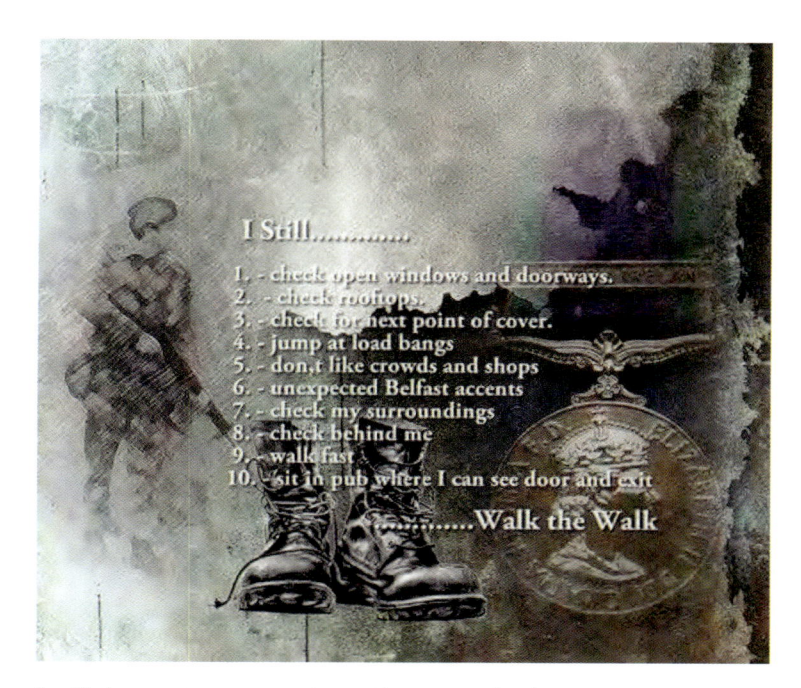

> I Still.............
> 1. - check open windows and doorways.
> 2. - check rooftops.
> 3. - check for next point of cover.
> 4. - jump at load bangs
> 5. - don,t like crowds and shops
> 6. - unexpected Belfast accents
> 7. - check my surroundings
> 8. - check behind me
> 9. - walk fast
> 10. - sit in pub where I can see door and exit
> ....Walk the Walk

I still do, as do many others I have no doubt.

We done our Duty a long time ago now, we were the guardians, we were professional soldiers, we kept our country safe. Every single one of us was proud to do so, when we meet up now on our annual re-unions, the numbers are slowly dwindling away, we always relive some part of one such event, .ie, a shooting or riot or I.E.D attack [contacts] or another story where we were outwitted by a bunch of baboons in Kenya robbing our food from the kitchen store. The laughter the tears and the comradeship will never stop. It does not matter if you are a rich accountant or you sweep roads for the local council, we are always, as we were then, equal. And in it together. We still have respect for each other. We do not talk about the bad things, those are personal and remain that way, not even our closest know about those and it will stay that way forever and rightly so. We just have to look each other in the eye and say nothing.

We have still a dress code for veterans, trousers, blazer, shirt and tie, with or sometimes without a beret, and still wear our medals with pride.

My first re-union, Norwich 2014, an emotional day.

Though probably not a best seller, I just wanted to get my story/memoirs in writing, the memory is fading now and the days when we were Kings is long gone, but if you have ever served and picked up a weapon for your Country, you will know, and hopefully relate to some of the contents of this book. Maybe it will stir a memory, or just bring a smile to your face, if so then great. If one of my Son,s Son,s happen to pick an old tattered copy up and a little smile appears, that would be great too.

All we ask is for a little respect, we have certainly earned it. Actually, a little more of that, along with manners, empathy and common decency in today,s crazy, fast moving world, would not go a miss.

The Government should also utilise our experience, and put it effect by way of Recruitment, where we are able to pass on our knowledge to new soldiers. At the moment, as previously mentioned, my Son has applied, and to be perfectly honest, the recruiting process is absolutely dreadful. Instead of passing it on to some civilian company, why not employ some of the Veterans to look after the new breed, we have all had the experience, and would definitely not let recruits, with no information or contact, for weeks, no encouragement or updates to their application, it truly is disgusting. I have heard that many who have applied actually have given up, because the process takes far too long, and these guys and gals just find another job, who can blame them, Yes, we do understand the medical scrutineering side of things, but the whole process takes too long. At time of writing I do indeed intend to look further into this matter and maybe write a few letters, to whom it may concern, time will tell, maybe the red tape and higher echelon people will sit up and take note.

We could also be used in the Local Cadet training, again passing on our knowledge helping the younger lads who wish to join. Yes, there has been debate about joining at 16 is too young, utter rubbish in my eyes, if you take a year to absorb all the information needed whilst still carrying on with your education then that has to be better than cramming the training into 16 weeks or whatever it may be now, never done me or my comrades whom all attended I.J.L.B Folkestone, any harm, I found it easier this way, and you have the chance to leave if it is not for you. Or use us in another capacity within Barracks, plenty of jobs we could do there from Stores jobs to Armoury, issuing weapons. Not sour grapes, just trying to make a point. Apart from my re-unions and phone calls to old comrades that is it for me. Loved every minute of serving.

Following Dad….

A short interruption.

We are now in July 2018, my son Ethan is about to follow in his Dads footsteps and will be going to the new Modern British Army very soon, currently awaiting his assessment day. He is so ready now and luckily for him he has more insight into the Army now than we had back then. The fitness alone required to join would alone be difficult for some to achieve, that is a mile and a half in 12 minutes!

He is currently flying around in under ten, Good Lad, we are similar in build, and he like me, loves the physical aspect of the job. He is destined for greater things in the military I am certain, but his journey is just beginning and I wish him the best of luck, although his application is held up[because he had a migraine once?] He will never give up.

This all started, when he was maybe five or six years old, I used to take him " up the woods" in fact it was like our own private training area, we would learn all the skills, camouflage and concealment , patrol techniques, making camp etc etc, covering pretty much most "in the field" training, and I kid you not, he is a natural.

He is well on the way now, and I will update his progress later in the book, by the time I have this completed he will probably be a Lance Jack![Lance Corporal].

We recently spoke about the new modern equipment mentioned earlier, he certainly knows how tough it will be, but am certain he will be ready for all of those challenges ahead, he has it already built in.

Ethan on patrol..

I have settled now, not far from where life began for me, Desborough, actually, approximately five miles from my old hometown of Rothwell, in Northamptonshire. Myself, Delilah my partner [common-law wife] I love so much, her Daughter Lottie, our 2 cats Sissy, and my mate Sox. My Son Ethan is over every couple of weeks. not for much longer, as he hopes to be following in the Old

Man,s footsteps. I am sure I gave him the bug to join, it must be in his D.N.A! Good Luck Son and enjoy the ride.

I have a job as a Transport Planner, for a small company based in Wellingborough, I believe twelve full time staff and four of those are our full time drivers, we all get on with the job in hand, and all in all, not a bad place to be, however the work can be quite hectic at times, but roll with it and prioritise as we go through the day.

Still full-time employment at -the -moment, however the back-problem, [degenerative spine] is worsening day by day, but still able to keep going. Morphine easing the pain at the minute, by the time this book goes into print I should know whether there is an operation available, to make the back pain more bearable, failing that it is spinal injections, either/or is fine by me as long as one of them is successful.

My partner Delilah is a hard- working carer in a Nursing Home, they all deserve medals by the way, however she is looking to management position at the home, or a complete change in direction, we have discussed and am sure she will decide shortly, good luck in whatever you chose babe. Lottie has now moved out and set up home with her new man, she has a great job in the local pharmacy, and as mentioned earlier Ethan will be following is old Dad in about 6 months . I figure like almost everyone else we budget and work to live, but to be honest, I have never been more contented.

Life is not bad at all, motoring on to 60 years old now, it is hard not being able to do the things you used to do, brain and heart says yes, body says a definite No! However, I am well looked after and in comparison with some of the heartache my old comrades have suffered, I am not doing too bad.

There is not one day goes by, without the Army popping up somewhere, through social media for instance, one of the guys posting about a holiday or some old pictures he found from back in the day.

Or on the National news, even a reminder whilst walking in town, Or, just in my head, you never forget! and why would we? We were proud, well trained and ready to die for our Country.

The training we received and some of the dreadful things we had to endure never stops, and is still useful to this day, if I feel down, which happens quite often now, all I have to do is conjure up one of the situations we were put in and Hey! Life is not so bad after all. Some of the memories make me sad and tearful but mostly a smile comes through, and believe me It is something very special to carry with you always. Back then it worked for us and it still works today, definitely -the -best trained Army is The British Army.

I will always miss it, still do, and did so for a few years until, through social media, was able to contact some of my old comrades, and am happy that I never lost touch with my life then, completely.

I hope you have enjoyed my short tale/memoirs of my 10 or so years in the Army in the Seventies and Eighties.

"ALL THE FOURS…THE POMPADOURS"…………………………

I must give special mention to the following, those whom assisted, changed, helped , trained, inspired, encouraged or generally were truly great soldiers and or friends;

In no particular order;

Monty B, Polly, Bob M, Billy E, Brian H, Fred B, Scratch, Gap, Dave N, Tony G, Titch W, A Steele, Spud Y, Andy C, Kev M, Steve Nev, You all know who you are so Thank you one and all.

Index to Abbreviations/Military wording;

NCO- Non - Commisioned Officer

L/Cpl – Lance Corporal

Cpl –Corporal

SGT – Sergeant

CSM – Company Sergeant Major

RSM – Regimental Sergeant Major

OC – Officer Commanding [Company]

CO – Officer Commanding [Battalion]

RP,s – Restriction of Priveleges

NAAFI – Navy, Army, Air Force Institute

FLAK JACKET – Protection Jacket [N.Ireland]

"Grotts" – Underwear/Boxers

FIBUA – Fighting in Built-Up A

"Choggy" Shop – On Camp café

"Nick" – Prison [In Barracks]

M.P -Military Police.

AWOL – Absent Without Leave

SLR – Self Loading Rifle

GPMG – General Purpose Machine Gun

84mm – Carl Gustav – Anti-Tank Weapon

66mm – Small anti-tank weapon

NBC – Nuclear Biological Chemical

"Thunderflash" – Stick-like Pyrotechnic

"Tin-Lid" – Steel Helmet

VCP – Vehicle Check Point

PIG – 1 Tonne Armoured Vehicle [N.Ireland]

SOPS – Standard Operating Procedure

FIBUA- Fighting in Built Up Areas

Exercise – Military Manouvres

Rtb – return to base

Brick – four man unit-N.I

BLURB………..

A Soldiers Tales from the 70,s and 80,s.

Bombings, Shootings and Peace-keeping but also heartfelt reflections to stoke the readers interest.

Reviving and reliving personal and collective memoirs over 10 years in The British Army.

From the Streets of West Belfast to the Jungle of Belize, from the Rocky landscapes of Malta to the Colchester Garrison.

After the Military, the change to Civilian Life..

Printed in Poland
by Amazon Fulfillment
Poland Sp. z o.o., Wrocław
18 December 2021